BECOMING
ENLIGHTENED

His Holiness the
Dalai Lama

BECOMING
ENLIGHTENED

Translated and edited by
Jeffrey Hopkins, Ph.D.

ATRIA BOOKS
New York   London   Toronto   Sydney

ATRIA BOOKS

A Division of Simon & Schuster, Inc.
1230 Avenue of the Americas
New York, NY 10020

First Atria Books hardcover edition January 2009

ATRIA BOOKS and colophon are trademarks of Simon & Schuster, Inc.

For information about special discounts for bulk purchases,
please contact Simon & Schuster Special Sales at
1-800-456-6798 or business@simonandschuster.com

Manufactured in the United States of America

1   3   5   7   9   10   8   6   4   2

ISBN-13: 978-1-4165-6583-3
ISBN-10:   1-4165-6583-3

Contents

Contents

Foreword

Tibet is renowned throughout the world for distilling the essence of Buddhist practice into easily comprehensible stages. In this book His Holiness the Dalai Lama lays out in an accessible and practical way the entire series of practices leading to enlightenment. After exploring Buddha's core teaching of interdependence, His Holiness shows how this fundamental insight leads to both a diagnosis of the human condition and the way out of the cyclic round of repeatedly moving from one life to the next, bringing our suffering with us. The Dalai Lama emphasizes the distinctive way Buddhist practices center around selflessness and seek to develop an altruistic attitude that promotes kindness and tolerance.

Formulated around a person's increasing spiritual capacity, the stages of spiritual training begin with recognizing the value of our present situation as humans and reflecting on the endowments that afford us such a marvelous opportunity for spiritual advancement. Within that appreciation, His Holiness explains the fragile nature of life and the nature of actions (karma) and their effects, as well as how to counteract the results of unhealthy deeds already committed.

The shift to a longer-range perspective—from concentrating on the pleasures of the moment to concern for the future—constitutes the first phase in transforming your spiritual perspective. A new outlook is wrought by recognizing that happiness needs to be achieved beyond the immediate moment, and from turning away from full involvement in the temporary and superficial toward the practice of virtue, which has both short-term and long-term benefits. Instead of seeking pleasure through the activities of accumulating wealth, power, and friends, you view virtues such as the practice of compassion as a better way to ensure a healthy future in the long run. The underpinning of this phase is to stop mistaking the present situation as permanent in order to open your horizon to consider what continues beyond the present. This moves us naturally to a discussion of death and rebirth, which contributes to a longer outlook.

The practices of middle-level training deepen this perspective by exploring what it means to want to be free from the seemingly endless cycle of death and rebirth. The thrust of this phase is to overcome an exaggerated sense of your own status, the status of others, and the status of objects of lust and hatred. Ignorance of the true nature of things is seen as the root cause of all our counterproductive emotions. The Dalai Lama explains how these harmful emotions arise and in what order, and lays out the problems they create through the impressions they leave in the mind: shaping our future experience, which results in our entrapment in a maelstrom of often unhealthy effects.

By taking account of the precariousness of your situation, you strengthen your resolve to seek rescue, through spiritual practice, from the entire uncontrolled round of birth, aging, sickness, and death. This change in outlook arises from penetrating the nature of appearances, not turning away from happiness, but recognizing a deeper happiness and the means to achieve it. This greater perspective impels us to meditate on interdependence and selflessness in order to undermine the ignorance on which our destructive emotions are built.

In the final section His Holiness paints a moving picture of the altruism that causes a practitioner to rise to the highest level of spiritual endeavor. You advance to this expanded spiritual capacity by extending your understanding of your own plight to others, realizing that they are in a similar situation. Here the emphasis is on developing totally unbiased compassion through a gradual series of cause-and-effect exercises. Ordinary concern and compassion are not replaced by otherworldly attitudes, but are extended far beyond their usual scope and are thereby transformed. The Dalai Lama focuses on how to produce, maintain, and increase this enlightened attitude while avoiding what undermines it. As with the earlier steps, the quest for happiness is not forsaken but is redirected to a higher goal, the shift here being an expansion of perspective so that the suffering of others becomes our primary concern.

The process of self-education and self-help presented in this book is first a withdrawal from the path of merely seeking superficial pleasures in the present moment, then from becoming entangled in afflictive emotions, and finally from self-centeredness. Through altruism that calls for the development of wisdom, His Holiness lays out the geography of this practice, and then, in the penultimate chapter, he presents insights into the true nature of reality. The meditative steps presented in this section gradually lead to direct realization of the true status of people and things so that our counterproductive attitudes can be removed and replaced by positive emotions. At the very end, His Holiness describes enlightenment in terms of the state of body, speech, and mind that is achieved through combining wisdom with the extraordinary power of altruism.

Throughout the pages that lie ahead, the Dalai Lama explains in intimate detail how each practice is generated, step by step. His unique approach is to interweave two core practices, compassion and the wisdom of selflessness, throughout the span of exercises. Since these practices are considered the two wings of a bird flying to enlightenment, he shows us their impact and relevance from the start. This is because, as he explains, the earlier and later practices influence and deepen each other. Thus these stages of spiritual practice are not rigid categories that require full realization of each step before the next; rather, they call for acquaintance with and repeated practice of the full gamut of exercises in order to allow cross-fertilization to take place.

The Dalai Lama's fascination with science and his three decades of interacting with international scientists have caused him to reframe basic Buddhist attitudes in terms of common approaches and attitudes, making this book highly accessible. In this way, all of us benefit from his thoroughgoing classical Tibetan education, a marvel of spiritual culture that the world so sorely needs.

Jeffrey Hopkins, Ph.D.
Emeritus Professor of Tibetan Studies
University of Virginia

BECOMING ENLIGHTENED

I

A Book About Enlightenment

We have arrived in the twenty-first century, a time of considerable material progress largely based on technological advances spurred on by a flurry of scientific discoveries. Nevertheless, the twentieth century was beset by a huge amount of violence, more than ever before, and at the start of the twenty-first century, murderous violence seems to be taking new forms, of ever-increasing power. This mess has been caused not by insufficient technical knowledge, nor by insufficient materials, but by an unruly mind.

While many in this world are enjoying increasing prosperity, many also remain in extreme poverty. In most countries there is a great disparity between social classes. Lacking wealth, the poor are terribly vulnerable. Consider, too, how many animals are being grown for slaughter, a number so great that the environment is being damaged.

These sad facts are due to insufficient loving care. If humanity's sense of caring for others increased, not only would people in the world be happier but the countless animals whose lives we directly affect would also have a better life. To increase our altruism we must motivate ourselves to take into consideration the effects of our actions on both the present and the future.

If unwanted suffering can be removed and happiness achieved merely through material advancement and wealth, then rich people should be free from suffering, but obviously this is not the case. In fact, once people obtain a good bit of money, comfort, and power, they tend to become excessively proud and jealous, particularly covetous, more focused on harm, and increasingly apprehensive. Those living in a moderate way are by no means impervious to the three poisons of lust, hatred, and ignorance, but for the most part they are bothered considerably less by additional problems.

What makes us unhappy? Our minds have fallen so far under the influence of self-destructive emotions that these attitudes, far from being viewed as harmful, are welcomed and promoted. That is what makes us squirm in discomfort.

If people could enjoy both external prosperity and inner qualities of goodness, outer and inner wealth, that indeed would provide a comfortable human life. Happiness does not come just from external circumstances; it mainly derives from inner attitudes. Nowadays those countries that have achieved great material progress are beginning to see that physical health and sickness, as well as the condition of society, are closely related to our mental processes.

Analytical investigation of the ways we think and feel are very important. Over the last three thousand years the most penetrating analysis of internal mental processes has occurred in India, so it is those insights that I draw on in this book to present in an easily accessible way the full range of practices leading to the enlightenment of Buddhahood.

IDENTIFYING BUDDHISM

Some 2,550 years ago, Buddha set forth a new religion in India. Some aspects of his ideas had already appeared there earlier, but no one had delineated these perspectives and techniques as conclusively as he would. What is at their core? Selflessness. Long before him, many had sought to analyze the status of the self, but not only did they teach that the self exists, they held that it exists independent of the mind and the body. However, Buddha concluded that when we assert that the self exists independently, our innate sense of self-centeredness increases and solidifies. As a result, the lust, anger, pride, jealousy, and doubt that stem from being self-centered grow stronger and more ingrained.

Seeing that defective states of mind such as lust and hatred are rooted in egotism, Buddha taught something that had not been explained before him, the view of selflessness. This was exceptional, and indeed for the more than 2,500 years that have passed since his time, no one outside of his tradition has taught this view.

As the Tibetan scholar Jamyang Shepa wrote near the end of the seventeenth century, "Non-Buddhist and Buddhist views derive from proving or refuting what is conceived by a view of self." In setting forth the view of selflessness, Buddha taught that a permanent unchangeable self, separate from mind and body, does not exist. Non-Buddhist schools not only accept such a self but seek to prove its independent existence through various approaches, whereas Buddhist systems seek to refute it.

It is not that the self is totally nonexistent; it is obvious that a self that desires happiness and does not want suffering does indeed exist. But Buddha taught that the self is set up in dependence upon the mind and body. In this way Buddha established the view known as dependent-arising, which emphasizes the interrelatedness of all things. Despite appearances to the contrary, nothing exists autonomously, or truly in isolation. All things have interconnections. The view of dependent-arising is Buddha's focal teaching.

Dependent-arising means that all phenomena—whether physical, mental, or otherwise—come into being based on certain causes and conditions. The happiness that the self seeks out and the suffering that the self seeks to remove do not arise independently but are produced by their own specific, temporary, appropriate causes. According to Buddhism they do not arise from permanent causes such as a permanent self-arisen Creator, or a permanent Nature, as was a popular belief in India. Buddha taught that phenomena arise *only* in dependence upon their respective causes and conditions. Everything is always in flux.

I am frequently asked what the Buddhist outlook is, and I respond by saying its view is dependent-arising, and its prescribed behavior is nonviolence. Nonviolence means to be motivated by compassion, which calls for helping others and, if that is not possible, then at least doing no harm. Dependent-arising and compassion are the essence of the Buddhist religion and the keys to its highest state: enlightenment.

2

Comparing Religions

When we compare the many religious teachers who have appeared in this world, we need to do this in terms of what they have taught, analyzing those areas in which they were particularly skilled; it is not sufficient merely to cite praises by their followers, for these are present in all religions. The process of comparison requires making differentiations, and in doing so we see that Buddha's doctrine is unique in seeing our apprehension of self as faulty and emphasizing that the antidote is the perspective of selflessness. In addition, Buddhism calls for bringing about the welfare of all sentient beings by transforming our usual attitudes toward self and others: we should refrain from self-cherishing and instead cherish others. In these ways Shakyamuni Buddha displays exceptional wisdom and compassion.

Buddha's emphasis on generating an altruistic intention to become enlightened by cherishing others rather than oneself and his emphasis on selflessness as an antidote to our mistaken views of the self make Buddhism distinctively deep. But would the world be better off if everyone became Buddhist? When Shakyamuni Buddha himself taught, not even all of India became Buddhist. If it were not necessary to speak to the dispositions and interests of his trainees, he could have taught the most profound system to all of them, but that is not the case; it is necessary that the doctrine be meaningful and useful for the individual trainee. Since the dispositions and interests of sentient beings are diverse, it was necessary even for Buddha to teach a wide variety of doctrines.

If the most profound doctrine—that all people and other phenomena are not established independently by way of their own character—is not meaningful for a trainee, a partial system of selflessness must be taught. Thus Buddha taught such students that people do not substantially exist but the mind-body complex does, thereby exempting it from the scope of selflessness. For those trainees for whom any level of the doctrine of selflessness could not for the time being fit in their minds, Buddha taught a modified doctrine of self, as when he said, "The mind-body complex is the burden; the bearer of the burden is the person."

In these ways, Buddha geared his teachings to the capacities of his students. If a teaching is not appropriate to a specific trainee, then even if the doctrine is correct, there is no way it can promote the well-being of the trainee. So for students for whom the doctrine of selflessness is not appropriate, a doctrine that fits their disposition and interest is better. From this perspective, we can clearly see that the many religious systems that have arisen in this world are beneficial to a great many beings.

It may be possible to discover which religion is the most profound, but if we ask which religious system is best, it is difficult to respond. The value of a religion is relative to each individual. A religion's philosophical view may be the most profound and comprehensive, but still it can be inappropriate for a particular individual. As I mentioned above, even to his followers Buddha did not always teach the most profound perspective. Rather than trying to force the deepest view on everyone, he taught according to individual interests and dispositions.

Thus even though the view that all phenomena are empty of independent existence may be the most profound, it is hard to say that it is the best. Teaching needs to be relevant to the student. For example, we may ask which medicine is the most valuable, and indeed there are medicines that are very expensive and others that are cheap. But if we ask which medicine is best, this entirely depends on the patient. If all sick people took the most expensive medicine, thinking it must be the best, it would harm some of them and not help others, whereas the least expensive could provide the most benefit for those in need of that specific treatment. Similarly, the value of a religious system depends on its relevance to the individual practitioner; whatever benefits that person most is best.

The question of value depends on the frame of reference, which for religious systems is primarily whether it helps or harms the practitioner. From this viewpoint, it cannot be said that Buddhism is the best in general, though it is the best for persons with a certain outlook and disposition. People need a system that fits them. This is why it is very important to value all religious systems. Although they have great differences philosophically, they all have precepts for cultivating a good attitude toward others and helping them, which means calling for the practice of love, compassion, patience, contentment, and appreciating the rules of society. Since all religions share these goals, it is important to respect them and value their contributions.

When we view philosophically based religions without bias, we clearly see that each has been beneficial for many people in the past, continues to be in the present, and will be in the future. Although a lot of problems have been caused in the name of the religions of this world, I believe they have helped more than they have harmed. When a call for better behavior is being heeded by a religion's followers, we should respect them, no matter whether their philosophical views are valid or not.

THE NEED FOR REASONING

According to an old Tibetan saying, we must value the person of a religious teacher but investigate the teaching. Even within Shakya-muni Buddha's teaching we need to distinguish between what requires interpretation and what is definitive, the distinction being made by reasoning. If a teaching of Buddha is contradicted by reasoning, it should not be taken literally, even though it is indeed his word. Similarly, when we look at the great beings who were Buddha's followers, it has to be said that certain teachings, such as those by the fourth-century Indian sage Asanga, which deny the existence of an external world that impinges on our senses, do not reflect reality. Although such teachings are to be found in certain of Buddha's scriptures, they do not necessarily represent his thinking. Again, this distinction between the thought of the scripture and the thought of the speaker can be determined by reasoning. That we have faith in Asanga does not require that we accept as literal the view of mind-only with a particular purpose in mind.

In the same way it is reasonable for Buddhists to respect the teachers of other religions. From one point of view, they could be emanations of a Buddha, and from another point of view, even if they are not emanations, their philosophies are helpful to certain people and may even be helpful to you at a certain juncture in your life.

Nevertheless, among adherents to any religion, including Buddhism, there are troublemakers. Though they might claim to be religious, they take doctrines that are intended to overcome lust, hatred, and bewilderment and instead mix them with their own afflictive emotions and misuse religion, making hard-and-fast distinctions between *us* and *them,* stirring up trouble. It seems to me that when adherents to a religion do this, it is not reasonable to say that this is the fault of the religion.

FAITH AND RESPECT

Since faith and respect are different, respect for other religions does not mean we must have faith in their doctrines. For example, I have met with some Christians who take interest in certain Buddhist practices, study them, and even practice them. They take particular interest in Buddhist methods for achieving one-pointed meditative concentration as well as how to increase love, compassion, and patience. Since these practices are common to Christianity and Buddhism, I express my admiration for what they are doing. To Christians, however, who have become interested in the view of emptiness, I lightheartedly respond that this is distinctively Buddhist and has little connection with Christian doctrine. Why? Probing emptiness requires looking into dependent-arising, and if its implications are understood, it becomes difficult to accept a single, permanent, unchangeable God as the creator of the world. If one tried to have faith in Christianity and in Buddhism, one would be asserting the existence of a Creator God and at the same time the nonexistence of a Creator God. That is impossible. Therefore, while *respect* is both feasible and beneficial, *faith* is another matter.

Among the many religions that assert a Creator God there are some followers who say that Buddhism is not a religion because it does not accept a God that created the world. Some of my Islamic friends, for instance, have told me that much of the advice found in Buddhism is very beneficial to people, including Muslims, but that many Muslims do not consider Buddhism to be a religion. Similarly, some strict Christians say that because Buddhists do not accept the existence a permanent self-arisen being, they are nihilists.

Once when I visited Canada, several Christian demonstrators carried signs saying they had nothing against me personally but that my philosophy was heretical. In Sweden, as I left my car one day I encountered a man carrying a sign. I put my palms together in a gesture of greeting, and he did the same. A journalist took a picture, which appeared in the newspaper the next day, celebrating that both the demonstrator and the object of demonstration were paying respect to each other. That indeed is how it should be, although I have to admit that I had not noticed that he was demonstrating against my views!

Indeed, from the viewpoint of religions that assert a Creator God, Buddhism has a philosophy of deprecation, seen in its denial of a Creator God, as well as a philosophy of exaggeration, seen in its assertion of former and future lives. Conversely, from a Buddhist viewpoint religions asserting a Creator God have a philosophy of exaggeration, as well as a philosophy of deprecation in their denial of the cause and effect of karma over the course of countless lifetimes.

Still, Buddhists need to recognize that for some people the assertion of a God who created everything brings a strong feeling of intimacy with God and draws them into accepting that they ought to behave in accordance with God's perspective. What is God's perspective? Love for everyone, helping others, altruism. For instance, Islam puts tremendous emphasis on helping others, especially the poor. The ninety-nine names of Allah, such as The Most Merciful, The Peace and Blessing, and The Loving and Kind One, revolve around love and sympathy. No religion describes a supreme being that is forever angry, always ferocious. No religion calls for its followers to be belligerent and to harm other people.

My point is that for some personality types the message that they should be warmhearted because there is a loving Creator God is more effective than the Buddhist message of relativity or relationality, which we call dependent-arising. Therefore, it is crucial to identify which religion is more beneficial for a particular person, given the great variety among people in terms of their disposition.

3

The Buddhist Framework

This book is titled *Becoming Enlightened* because it teaches the stages of the path to full realization of our potential. "Enlightenment" is what is to be arrived at, accomplished, attained. The techniques for proceeding to enlightenment are called the path, which is set forth in stages to clarify the order of their practice, ranging from what a beginner should do on up to the ultimate attainment of perfection.

Many Buddhist texts are organized around three central topics: the status of phenomena, the practices for spiritual progress, and the effects of those practices. We call these three the basis, the path, and the fruit. The notion is that if you use certain principles as the foundation of your practice, there are advantages to be accrued, and if you implement these tenets, the fruits of your practice will help fulfill your purposes.

What are the paths, the practices, for actualizing the great enlightenment? Morality, concentrated meditation, and wisdom, enhanced by compassion. All Buddhist systems have compassion at their root. In the morality of abandoning the ten nonvirtues—the three physical nonvirtues (killing, stealing, and sexual misconduct), the four verbal nonvirtues (lying, divisive talk, harsh speech, and senseless chatter), and the three mental nonvirtues (covetous-ness, harmful intent, and wrong views)—the prohibition against killing includes not just humans but all living beings; it is not suit-able to harm any living being. This is due to the fact that the very foundation of Buddhism is compassion.

Among the many forms of Buddhism, there is a group of sys-tems in which compassion goes beyond empathy and extends to committing yourself to relieve the sufferings of all sentient beings throughout space. This high resolve, which is intentionally culti-vated to the point of seeking enlightenment for the sake of bring-ing about the welfare of others, is called the "altruistic intention to become enlightened." When morality, concentrated meditation, and wisdom are practiced within this attitude, you can attain the enlightenment of a Buddha. This is the path to enlightenment.

THE PATH

The core practices of Buddhism are the *profound view* of dependent-arising and of emptiness and the *vast deeds* of compassion. The prac-tice of insight is called "profound" because it does not take place on the superficial level of appearances, but is based on the way things really are, on their mode of being. When you are not satisfied with the surface but seek the inner nature of things through investiga-tion and analysis, you discover their true nature, which is empty of independent, or inherent, existence.

The term *view* can, according to context, refer to the conscious-ness of the viewer, or to the act of viewing, or to the object that is being viewed. The "profound view" of Buddhism often refers to the last of these: the subtle status of phenomena that is viewed, or real-ized, with wisdom. This is why the first set of core practices, the profound view of dependent-arising and of emptiness, has come to be called the "stages of the path concerned with the profound."

The other set of core practices, the vast deeds of compassion, is called "vast" because its many paths, levels, and so on are practiced with all the tools at our disposal—body, speech, and mind. These are the "stages of the path concerned with vast deeds."

THE TRANSMISSIONS OF THESE CORE PRACTICES

In India, the stages of the path concerned with the profound were primarily transmitted through the Indian sage Nagarjuna, who lived around the first and second century c.e., whereas the stages of the path concerned with the vast deeds of compassion were mainly transmitted through the Indian sage Asanga, mentioned above. Though both of these great figures practiced the full complement of profound and vast paths, their individual interests caused them to emphasize particular aspects of the path. Nagarjuna emphasized delineating emptiness in his *Six Collections of Reasonings,* whereas Asanga's emphasis was on the paths and stages of spiritual practice, as described in his *Five Treatises on the Grounds.*

The profound view of emptiness and the vast deeds of compassion transmitted by these two great figures, Nagarjuna and Asanga, are the principal topics of this book. Tibet was fortunate to have the full scope of Buddhist systems, ranging from those for persons aiming mainly at their own enlightenment to those more altruistically oriented methods called the Great Vehicle. I will explain the stages of the path to enlightenment keeping all of these practices in mind; they culminate in the achievement of altruistic omniscience.

CLASSIFYING BUDDHIST TEXTS

Buddhist texts in general fall into three classes—science, philosophy, and religion. Buddhist science concerns the basic status of phenomena, while Buddhist philosophy details the implications of that status. Then, based on this Buddhist science and philosophy, we see extensive Buddhist spiritual practices, which are aspects of religion.

For more than three decades I have had contact with international scientists. Here the relationship is with Buddhist science, which concerns the basic status of phenomena as expressed in texts such as Vasubandhu's *Treasury of Manifest Knowledge*, where there is considerable discussion of cosmology, the basic elements, minute particles, and so on; it also concerns the rich teachings of Buddhist psychology, including neurological information, detailing nerve pathways and the energy coursing through them. These topics of Buddhist science are the basis for my exchanges with modern science, along with my own belief that Buddhist sciences can benefit a great deal from contemporary international science.

It would be foolish for Buddhists to claim that the traditions we already have are sufficient. International science is amazingly deep on these topics, which are presented in terms of measurement and calculation, and I believe it is very beneficial for Buddhists to study these. International science also has a great deal to learn from Buddhist science, especially psychology. An Indian scholar such as Vasubandhu would find much to learn from contemporary international science about cosmology and the like, but it seems to me that Nagarjuna, who was more interested in the workings of the mind, would not have to alter his science or philosophy in the slightest.

4

Practicing Buddhism

Practicing the Buddhist religion mainly means improving the mind. In Tibetan the word for "religion" is *chö*, which means to adjust, to improve, to change for the better. The basic idea is to transform that which produces pain, to overcome our unruly attitudes. In Sanskrit the term for "religion" is *dharma*, which means to hold back, that is to say, to protect ourselves from unwanted suffering by developing antidotes to the causes of that suffering. For instance, by adopting the virtue of abandoning killing you prevent the mis-deed of murder, thereby protecting yourself from the effects of murder, which are infelicitous rebirth, short life, and the like.

Through practice you develop antidotes for the unfavorable activities of body, speech, or mind, and by doing so you protect yourself from the sufferings that they would produce. Religion in this context comprises 1) the antidotes for destructive emotions and 2) freedom from those destructive emotions and their effects. In Buddhism, this is the basis of religion.

How can we transform attitudes? They cannot be changed by external laws, police, or armies. Consider the attempts to impose Marxism and Leninism on the Russian and Chinese people; they were failures. Then how *is* transformation accomplished? By internal, voluntary, and enthusiastic effort. Physical and verbal behavior can temporarily be controlled by an external force; for example, even a talkative student will sit quietly in front of an irascible teacher. However, long-lasting change comes only from within, from your own interest, not from external control.

To be motivated this way, you need to see the value of change and the disadvantages of not changing. This means knowing that if you are guided by an unruly mind you will be uncomfortable in the short run and will truly suffer in the long run, and that if you are guided by a tamed mind you will be happier in the short term and will profoundly benefit in the long term—helping both yourself and those around you. By seeing the disadvantages of unruly attitudes, you will avoid them, and by seeing the advantages of tamed attitudes, you will voluntarily wish to adopt them. These choices are made through analytical thinking.

THE NEED FOR AN UNBIASED OUTLOOK

To analyze something effectively, you need to be unbiased. If you are prejudiced so that from the outset you are committed to one side of an issue or the other, then when you analyze, the results will be twisted. You need to start within an attitude free from seeing one notion as good and the other as bad, and instead be willing to entertain the possibility that either notion could be good or bad. By analyzing without bias you will be capable of seeing advantages and disadvantages.

As the Tibetan sage Tsongkhapa, who lived in the late fourteenth and early fifteenth centuries, put it, "If you are partisan, you will be obstructed by bias and will not recognize the actual advantages." This is why it is crucial to be unbiased and willing to face whatever the reality of a situation may be. For this you need to begin with doubt; from doubt you will question; from questioning you will analyze; from analysis the truth will become clear, and whatever is untrue will fade. Doubting induces questioning, which induces analysis, which induces ascertainment. In this process, doubt is crucial.

Nagarjuna's student Aryadeva calls for a practitioner to have three qualities: lack of bias, intelligence, and aspiration. Bias keeps us from seeing reality; lack of intelligence prevents analysis; and lack of aspiration prevents implementation. Thus once you have successfully avoided partisanship, use your intelligence to examine doctrines and practices and then implement what you have determined is beneficial. If you try to launch into Buddhist practice with a preconceived notion that Buddhism is really great, it will be difficult to go deep; you must act from a knowledge of facts as you yourself truly see them.

DAILY PRACTICE

Spiritual practice includes what we do in meditative sessions and what we do between sessions; the entire twenty-four-hour day is involved. When you rise in the morning, if you are a Buddhist, you should think:

I am spending my life as a full-fledged follower of Buddha. May I remove the three poisons of lust, hatred, and ignorance! Destructive emotions, of course, will arise, but I will not voluntarily rush into them. Today I will do whatever I can to read texts, reflect on their meaning, and work at developing wisdom. I will also do whatever I can to generate the altruistic intention to become enlightened and implement compassion in my behavior. May whatever obstructs the generation of these practices be pacified!

This thinking will set up a virtuous attitude for the entire day. Then you can begin the activities of your day, including having a nice breakfast! Make offering of whatever you eat or drink to the Buddha and the other great figures who teach the path to enlightenment.

Since the mind is drawn into lust for pleasant objects and into hatred for the unpleasant, it is important to control your senses by keeping away from those places where such destructive emotions are generated; this means choosing an isolated place for practice, if possible. At those times when your senses encounter pleasant and unpleasant objects, practice keeping your mind from falling into lust and hatred.

You need to identify that both lust and hatred are self-destructive emotions by recognizing their disadvantages; determine not to sanction them. Then, mindful that these emotions need to be restrained, use introspection to see whether you are encountering objects and situations that might generate lust or hatred. When such objects and situations are present, see if afflictive emotions are being generated. You need to keep this up no matter what you are doing. As the sage Tsongkhapa says, "When engaging in any action—physical, verbal, or mental—do it within being aware of what is suitable and not suitable to do." Mindfulness and introspection cultivated during everyday activities will prepare these faculties to be of service during meditation, which cannot occur without them.

At the end of the day, review whether your activities accorded with your motivation, taking joy in those that went well and did not contradict your intentions. Regarding those that went less well, consider your mistakes without hiding them, disclose them to yourself, and develop an intention not to engage in them in the future. Having corrected yourself and urged yourself on, go to sleep while bringing to mind virtuous attitudes such as faith, compassion, the altruistic intention to become enlightened, and the view of emptiness as much as you can; in this way even sleep can be turned in a virtuous direction. Sleep is affected by motivating forces just prior to it, be they virtuous, nonvirtuous, or neutral. Hence it is important to manifest a virtuous attitude before sleeping.

In this way, you can make use of each day of your life, while recognizing that lust and hatred continue to arise intermittently. This keeps you from becoming discouraged.

How to Study

In general, when starting any type of helpful study, if you look into its benefits, including its purpose and possible results, you will develop a strong wish to carry it out. The same is true for the study of religious doctrines and practices. If you recognize their benefits, you will be enthusiastic about starting to study and about continuing once you have begun.

What are the benefits of Buddhism? Through studying the training in morality you will learn what you need to adopt in your daily behavior and what you need to discard, thereby turning yourself away from ill deeds. Then, through studying the training in concentrative meditation you will learn how to avoid having your mind be too loose or too tight, so you will be able to set your mind and stay on a topic without being distracted. Then, through studying the training in wisdom you will become able to penetrate the meaning of selflessness. By concentrating on selflessness you will overcome ingrained misunderstanding of the nature of people and things, which is the root of the round of repeated birth, aging, sickness, and death (what Buddhists call "cyclic existence"), and you will attain liberation from suffering.

In this way, listening to teachings and studying them is:

- like a *lamp*, dispelling the darkness of ignorance;
- the supreme form of *wealth*, since unlike external possessions it does not attract thieves, muggings, and even untimely death;
- the best of *weapons*, in that by removing counterproductive emotions the foe of ignorance is eventually vanquished;
- the best of *friends*, since when you study altruism you learn various techniques for helping others through the practices of giving, morality, and patience, as well as how to attract and treat students;
- the best of *companions*, since listening to and studying teachings generates internal qualities that remain unchanged whether your external comforts increase or diminish;
- harmless *medicine*, since this internal development will never turn against you, unlike ordinary medicine, which can harm you under certain conditions, such as when you take pills that you do not need;
- an *army*, defeating your own afflictive emotions and karmas (actions) impelled by them;
- the best *fame, glory, and treasure*, for through them the most favorable forces for your future are achieved;

- the best of *gifts*, because they will cause you to recognize these qualities of character and respect them.

The purpose of listening to and studying Buddhist doctrines is to overcome the three poisonous afflictive emotions—lust, hatred, and ignorance—and to engage in altruistic practices so you can achieve an all-knowing state that will enable you to help others on a vast scale. Therefore, once you have listened to these teachings, it is crucial to implement them according to your capacity, whereby you can eventually attain release from the prison of rebirth.

When you read or listen to such beneficial advice, it is important to set aside pride and attend to the teachings respectfully. As Buddha said, "Listen well, thoroughly, and keep the teaching in mind." If, when listening to a lecture, your mind is elsewhere, then this is like filling an upside-down vessel, for the teaching is not entering your mind. If later you forget what you have heard, this is like filling a leaky vessel; it is not staying in your mind. Take written notes if that helps.

Even if this teaching goes into your ears and stays in your mind, if you use it for superficial purposes such as gaining income or fame, it will not be beneficial. What could have been helpful has been corrupted by a faulty motivation, like a dirty vessel polluting whatever is poured into it.

Buddhist doctrine can help you realize a state free from afflictive emotions. Because you are seeking to resolve your own problems, picture yourself as a sick person who has come under the influence of three destructive diseases: lust, hatred, and ignorance. Your teacher is like a doctor who knows how to counteract these unfavorable forces, and what you are being taught is like medicine.

That medicine has to be taken. To be cured of a disease it is not sufficient to merely procure the medicine or know how it works; you have to ingest it. Similarly, to be cured of poisonous destructive emotions you have to implement the techniques for removing those poisons. The methods have to be taken to mind, and the mind has to become one with the practices.

In general, when you study topics such as grammar or history, you need only register the points being made; however, when you study topics whose aim is mental improvement, it is necessary to mix your mind with the meaning of the lessons. If you treat teachings that offer methods for training your mind as just part of an enumeration of what is knowable, you will miss their impact. You need to constantly apply these methods and insights to your own experience so that even if you read only a page of lessons, feeling is evoked, and your mind is moved. Otherwise, even if you become familiar with the teachings in an external way, they will not help. You may become proud and even jealous—a haughty and pugnacious scholar! Such a faulty result would show that your own attitudes have not become intertwined with the teachings.

From the start, treat the teachings as guidance, or advice. As Tsongkhapa says in his *Great Treatise on the Stages of the Path*:

> When you listen to the teachings, if you set your own mental continuum off separately and treat the teachings as something divorced from them, then no matter what is explained, it will not be effective. Listen to the teachings in order to determine the condition of your own mindstream. For example, when you want to know whether or not there is dirt or the like on your face, you find out by looking in a mirror and then remove the stain. Similarly, when you listen to the teachings, the faults

that have developed in your behavior appear in the mirror of the teachings, and you will generate a sense of discomfort, "My mind has become like this!" Then you will work to clear away those faults and achieve favorable qualities.

When you choose not to accept self-destructive emotions but want to cleanse yourself of such problems, you will see that Buddhist techniques are effective, and you will naturally generate within yourself more and more interest in them. You will want these techniques to grow and develop in your own mind, and in the minds of others.

Meditation

There are two types of meditation: one that involves analysis and another that involves just placing the mind single-pointedly on an object without any analysis. The first is called analytical meditation, and the second is known as stabilizing meditation. Some people think that meditation is merely a matter of not thinking much, but that is only one type; needless to say, it differs greatly from analytical meditation!

Since meditation in general means familiarization, analytical meditation means to familiarize oneself with a topic by way of examination and investigation. By contrast, stabilizing meditation means to simply set your mind with great alertness on a single point at which you have arrived through analysis. In stabilizing meditation, you become more familiar with an object or a perspective by focusing your mind on it after making a decision to do so; you are keeping your mind within a specific state, without engaging in further investigation.

Analytical meditation is crucial. It is not sufficient just to promise to transform your mind or to wish to do so; that alone will not succeed. To improve your mind, you need to think a lot about the reasons for doing so, coming to know them from the very depths of your mind, which will motivate strong aspiration and effort. For instance, when you are cultivating compassion, a prayerful wish that all sentient beings be free from suffering and the causes of suffering is helpful, but it is not enough; you need to reflect on the reasons for this compassion from many viewpoints, as I will explain in chapters 15 and 16.

Let me tell you about a system of nonreflective meditation from ancient Tibet. In the eighth century at Samye Monastery, south of Lhasa, the capital, there were four temple complexes: the Sanctuary of Pure Morality, where the Indian master Shantarakshita, as abbot, transmitted monastic vows to seven persons whose predispositions for Buddhist practice had awakened; the Sanctuary of Translation, for scholar-translators; the Sanctuary of Immovable Concentration, where a Chinese tradition of Chan was practiced; and the Sanctuary of Mantrika Practitioners Taming Demons, for ordained lay practitioners of Tantra. In the Sanctuary of Immovable Concentration monks from China only practiced nonconceptual meditation, which eventually turned into not bringing anything at all to mind. At that time, many spiritually minded Tibetans felt that all kinds of conceptualization were problematic and sought, like these Chinese monastics, to stop all thought. Shantarakshita's student Kamalashila refuted this approach in a famous debate at Samye and through a trilogy called *Stages of Meditation.*

It is likely that in China the origins of this focus on nonconceptualization were in a tradition of study and contemplative thinking performed prior to meditation, and then, when realization of selflessness was cultivated at the level of real experience, they concentrated one-pointedly on selflessness in meditation. However, in time "nonconceptual" came to mean "not taking anything to mind." Kamalashila did not accept this meaning, emphasizing the importance of analytical meditation, as did the later Tibetan sage Tsongkhapa in his *Great Treatise on the Stages of the Path.*

THE NEED FOR ANALYSIS

In Buddhism in general and in the tradition stemming from the great monastic schools of India in particular, faith relies on conclusions that come from analysis. Similarly, compassion is engendered by analyzing our situation in the world in relation to others. Also, the wisdom that realizes impermanence comes by way of analysis, as does the wisdom that realizes selflessness. An analytical attitude is important at the beginning, middle, and even the end of the spiritual path, since for wisdom to fully mature in Buddhahood you need from the outset to enthusiastically investigate the nature of things and to develop this attitude more and more.

It is not sufficient to think "Buddha said so," or "My Lama said so." Notice how much reasoning and debate there is in the texts by Nagarjuna, Aryadeva, Chandrakirti, Shantideva, Shantarakshita, and Kamalashila. Analysis and reflection lead to conviction, which in turn yields a strong commitment to change your outlook and attitude; then, with familiarization, or meditation, your mind will gradually be transformed.

In this way intelligence is a prerequisite for the practice of Buddhism. By making use of your full range of intellect you can adjust and transform a wide range of emotions. By reasoning rather than just fixing your mind on a topic, you form valid cognition, and through its force erroneous attitudes gradually unravel. For this, mere scholarship is not sufficient; what is needed is implementation at the level of deep feeling, full-fledged meditation.

SUBJECTIVE AND OBJECTIVE MEDITATION

There are two main styles of meditation: meditating on a subjective aspect and meditating on an objective aspect. When we speak of "meditating faith" or "meditating compassion," this refers to cultivating the subjective attitudes in meditation, causing your mind to become faithful or compassionate. However, when we speak of meditating on impermanence or selflessness, these topics are the focus of objective meditation. There are still other kinds of meditation, such as "imaginative meditation," which might involve meditating on a space filled with skeletons in order to diminish lust; here you are not truly thinking that the area is actually cluttered with decomposed bodies; you are using imagination for the specific purpose of putting lust in a larger perspective. There is also "reflective meditation," in which you bring to mind qualities of higher levels of the path, such as great compassion and the realization of emptiness. In your mind you run through a whole range of practices, taking each to mind even though you have not yet arrived at the higher levels; this type of meditation helps to pave the way for later realization.

WHEN TO MEDITATE

If possible, meditate in four sessions every day—dawn, morning, afternoon, and evening. At a minimum, establish a regular pattern of daily meditation. For those holding down a job it may only be possible to meditate in the morning or evening. Most people find that the mind is clearer in the morning, so meditating every morning may be preferable; I find my mind is clearer in the early morning. As to the length of the session, until you are well used to the process, it is best to meditate in brief sessions of only several minutes, gradually lengthening the period of time. During vacations you can lengthen and increase the number of sessions.

5

Knowing the Qualifications
of a Teacher

In general a teacher is useful for gaining knowledge, and it is particularly important for a teacher of spiritual topics to be properly qualified. Chief among these qualifications are expertise in the spiritual texts and direct experience of what is being taught. Since the very purpose of Buddhist learning is to discipline the mind, a teacher of such knowledge could not help tame anyone else's mind without first having tamed her own. Therefore, a teacher must herself possess inner qualities of experiential realization and scriptural understanding surpassing those of her students.

How is that accomplished? Through the three trainings in morality, meditative concentration, and wisdom. Specifically, whether you have taken monastic vows or you are a layperson, as a teacher you should have sufficient training in morality such that your senses are controlled. Otherwise your senses will be like wild horses, pulling you into unfit actions. Also, you need to have experience in one-pointed meditative concentration so that you can overcome distractions such as external excitation and internal dullness. Furthermore, you need the wisdom of selflessness, and specifically of the emptiness of inherent existence, in order to thoroughly pacify counterproductive emotions that make your mental continuum intractable. At a minimum, you need some familiarity with selflessness by way of scriptures and reasoning.

To teach trainees it is necessary to have a wealth of scriptural knowledge as well as acquaintance with and understanding of a range of teachings, so that when teamed with skill in techniques of instruction you can stimulate understanding in students. To accomplish this, you need to be energetically enthusiastic about improving the welfare of your students, to have only loving sympathy for them, and to forgo any personal concern about the hardships involved in explaining doctrines over and over again until they can sink in.

Just as it is important for those who want to be teachers to work at gaining these qualities, so it is important for students to understand the attributes of a good spiritual teacher and to try to find someone endowed with them. If you cannot find anyone who has all of these attributes, at least find someone who has more good qualities than defects; avoid those whose defects predominate or who are in the same situation as you.

There are Tibetans in various parts of the world who are attempting to teach but are not qualified to do so. Students need to take care in order to avoid such teachers. Rushing headlong into this venture is inappropriate. Analyze first. Just as a teacher needs the power of analysis to become learned, so does a student need analysis from the very start. Buddhist doctrines aim at providing antidotes to the three poisons of lust, hatred, and ignorance; for this, discriminating wisdom is needed.

Kunu Lama Tenzin Gyaltsen once told me a story about Paltrul Rinpoche, a great lama from the southeast province of Tibet called Kham. An upholder of the tradition of Shantideva's *A Guide to the Bodhisattva's Way of Life,* Paltrul Rinpoche was a true monastic and lived very simply. Once, when he was visiting an area, many students had gathered around him, and many local people had come to have an audience with him. A bit fed up with all the fuss, he went off on his own to another village, where he asked a family for a place to stay. The mother of the family took him on as a servant, where he swept the floor and performed other chores, including emptying the nightly urine pots. After a number of days several monks arrived there, inquiring of the lady of the house whether their lama was staying anywhere in the vicinity. She asked for a description of him, which they provided, whereupon she understood what she had done and was completely embarrassed.

Real lamas like Paltrul Rinpoche assume a humble posture, even though they are endowed with tremendous qualities of character. In Sanskrit the word for lama is *guru,* which literally means "heavy" in the sense of being possessed of many great qualities leading to altruistic activities. Nowadays, many so-called lamas have lost sight of this; the height of their teaching thrones and the elegance of their special hats do not reflect their inner state.

If you find a qualified teacher, you will value her; the best way to do this is to achieve what she teaches.

HOW TO TEACH

The person explaining Buddhist doctrine should be motivated purely by a desire to help. One of the early Tibetan teachers in the Kadam tradition said that he had never lectured on doctrines without having first meditated for a period on impermanence, and this is a good example of just how crucial it is for a teacher to adjust his motivation before starting. Teaching cannot be undertaken with an aim to obtain goods, services, or fame. When you lecture out of a wish to receive gifts in return, it is like selling the doctrine for a price. This is really terrible; far from helping, it is actually harmful. Though your teaching performance might look nice on the outside, on the inside you are seeking refuge in acquisitiveness. As the Tibetan master Geshe Sharapa said:

> We use the word "guru" for whoever is pleased by a student's practice and does not give even the slightest consideration to material gifts. One who does the opposite is not suitable to be a guru for those wishing to achieve liberation.

In the seventeenth century, Tsele Rangdrol, a lama from the Great Completeness tradition of the Nyingma sect of Tibetan Buddhism, reported that he had decided to give up traveling by horse, give up eating meat, and never accept offerings for teaching doctrine. When I read his biography, I came to a decision not to accept offerings when I give lectures around the world, insisting that offerings and entrance fees be used for the organizers' expenses, and when there is anything left over, that it be given to charity.

If you are a teacher, before sitting down to teach imagine your own teacher on the place from which you will be speaking and bow down three times, thereby showing reverence for the source of your teachings and for the teachings themselves. Before I ascend the platform from which I lecture, I imagine my main teacher, Ling Rinpoche, sitting on that seat, and I bow down to him; then, just as I am sitting down, I recite to myself the words of the *Diamond Cutter Sutra* about impermanence:

> View things compounded from causes
> To be like twinkling stars, figments seen with an eye disease,

The flickering light of a butter-lamp, magical illusions,
Dew, bubbles, dreams, lightning, and clouds.

I reflect on the evanescence of phenomena and on selflessness, and then I snap my fingers, the brief sound symbolizing impermanence. This is how I remind myself that I will soon be descending from the high throne, thereby avoiding self-inflation.

A teacher should view himself or herself like a doctor, with the teachings as medicine, and those listening as patients in need of medicine. Also, the act of explaining the doctrine should be undertaken without any sense of looking down on the audience; it cannot be performed out of a desire to put down others and raise yourself up. By considering yourself and those listening one and the same, you are conveying the doctrine as it connects to your experience within an overarching attitude of love. Make sure to avoid jealous fears that others might be spiritually higher than you, procrastination (putting off teaching to another time), discouragement from having to repeat points again and again, holding back what you know, and making claims about yourself and finding fault with others. Within this outlook, teaching with a true sense of altruism is indeed beneficial. Moreover, it will help you achieve enlightenment so that you can be of even greater help to others; such teaching is a path to realizing your own deepest happiness.

Before teaching, wash, and put on clean clothes. Then, in a clean and appealing place begin the lecture by reciting the *Heart Sutra* to keep away interfering factors. Teach with a bright, cheerful countenance using examples, reasons, and scriptural citations. Avoid confusing things by taking a little from here and a little from there; refrain from speaking only about the easy points and leaving the more difficult without explanation; and avoid teaching what you have not ascertained, whose meaning you have merely guessed at.

Once you determine that it would indeed be beneficial, teach those who, with pure motivation and great aspiration, approach you and request teaching. Otherwise, it is unsuitable to put yourself forward and try to teach whomever you meet. From a Buddhist viewpoint, proselytizing is not appropriate, for once a religion seeks to convert people, then other religions will do the same, which will lead to competition and likely to trouble. When I give lectures in the West, I tell the audience that generally speaking it is better if they stay with the religion of their parents, which is usually Christianity, Islam, or Judaism. As we have discussed, practitioners of these religions can sometimes benefit from Buddhist doctrines and practices, but generally it is good if people stick to the religion they grew up with.

At the conclusion of a teaching, the lecturer and the listeners together should dedicate the virtue of the session to the welfare of all sentient beings. If you are able to do so, also reflect on how all phenomena, such as the teaching session itself, are illusions in the sense that they appear to exist independently but do not; rather, they depend on an array of factors. This seals the experience within a true understanding of its nature, and of the nature of all things.

6

Buddhism in India and Tibet

Shakyamuni Buddha is said to be the fourth of a thousand Buddhas to appear in this era. According to our texts, the three previous Buddhas in this era appeared when the average life span of humans was eighty thousand years, sixty thousand years, and twenty thousand years, respectively. When we examine this in the light of current scientific thinking, this legendary history may need to be reconsidered. Just as those Christians who assert that only five or ten thousand years have passed since the creation of this world find themselves at odds with scientific evidence of human skeletons from millions of years ago, so we Buddhists have a problem with our texts positing too long a period since the development of humans in this world. Our books speak of humans appearing long before even the three earlier Buddhas, so we need to reconsider this account in the light of Darwin's theory of evolution.

Buddhists have to admit that there are contradictions between where our texts, such as Vasubandhu's *Treasury of Manifest Knowledge*, physically place certain realms of rebirth, and scientific measurements of our planet. To deny such evidence would be to contradict what is directly observed, and since it is a basic principle of Buddhist philosophy not to contradict reasoning, we of course cannot contradict direct observation. Thus the measurements that are set forth in certain Buddhist texts cannot be taken literally.

In any case, Buddha's teaching is divided into scriptural and realizational teachings, the latter being the three trainings— morality, concentrated meditation, and wisdom. Through scriptural teachings you learn how to generate the three trainings in your mind stream, after which you can practice them and eventually realize them. Since in order to practice you need to know how to do so, scriptural teachings come first. Great Buddhist figures of the past listened to a vast number of teachings, thereby developing vast knowledge. By putting into practice what they had heard and studied, they realized these teachings directly, in the form of experiences.

NALANDA

Over the course of centuries, Buddha's teachings were transmitted down through the scholar-yogis of the great Buddhist institution of learning called Nalanda, which was the most important and famous institute in India for apprehending, maintaining, and advancing the systems of the entire range of Buddha's teachings. This center of learning reached its peak under the leadership of Nagarjuna. Most of the great Buddhist authors of Sanskrit texts were Nalanda scholars, and later when another great center, Vikramalashila, formed, it used Nalanda's texts and methods of study, with minor variations.

The great Indian figures from whom the four major Tibetan sects derive—Shantarakshita and Padmasambhava for the Old Translation sect of Nyingma, Virupa for the Sakya sect, Naropa for the Kagyu sect, and Atisha for the Geluk sect—were all great scholars at Nalanda or its derivative Vikramalashila, and thus it is clear that all of the religious orders in the snowy land of Tibet maintain a lineage from Nalanda.

As the great Indian teacher Vasubandhu said, becoming an appropriator, maintainer, and disseminator of the realizational teachings depends on practice—there is no other way. In Chinese Buddhism, there are followers of Pure Land traditions who read Buddha's teachings about the benefits of rebirth in a Pure Land and focus their most fervent prayers on being born there. In China and Tibet there are meditators who strive to generate single-pointed meditative concentration without paying much attention to book learning. But according to Nalanda's process, it is important to engage in considerable study *and* to implement whatever you have understood from study, in the tradition of exposition first and then implementation. (Sometimes Tibetans place their emphasis on building temples and religious monuments but engage in neither study nor practice to further their own welfare. Although it is good to build temples, it should not be the primary religious activity.)

STAGES OF THE PATH LITERATURE

The most significant introduction to Tibet of the traditions of the profound view and the vast compassionate deeds occurred in the eighth century C.E. through Shantarakshita, who himself was Nalanda-educated and was invited to Tibet by King Trisong Detsen. During that same historic period, the Indian master Padmasambhava was also renowned for removing obstacles in Tibet to the spread of Buddhist doctrines. Therefore, these three—the expert Shantarakshita, the master Padmasambhava, and the patron King Trisong Detsen—are celebrated as the triad who laid the foundation of Buddhism in Tibet. Buddhism had already spread to China starting seven hundred years earlier.

In the eleventh century the Indian scholar-yogi Atisha, who was born in Bengal in a royal family and whose home institution of learning was Vikramalashila, came to Tibet. Since by the time Atisha arrived in Tibet, the country was almost entirely Buddhist, he did not need to first refute other systems, or to defend these doctrines and views. Given the dispositions and interests of the Tibetan people as well as their somewhat isolated physical environment, what they needed was an ordered structure of practical instructions, so Atisha composed a text titled *Lamp for the Path to Enlightenment*.

In India, convention called for ordering the stages of spiritual practice into three levels of increasing capacity. Using this tradition as his source, Atisha presented Tibetans with three stages of implementation: first lesser capacity, then middling capacity, and finally great capacity. These three degrees are based on the fact that all of Buddha's teachings are intended to help beings accomplish desirable temporary and ultimate goals. The temporary goal is good life within cyclic existence conducive to spiritual practice, and the final aim is liberation from cyclic existence and the achievement of altruistic omniscience.

In terms of what these three levels of practitioners are seeking to overcome, there are three levels of suffering:

1. *Outright physical and mental pain* (from headaches to back pain to sore feelings).
2. *Suffering from change.* Most ordinary pleasures are based on relief from pain, for example, when you sit down after walk-

ing too long; they are not pleasurable in and of themselves. However, we mistake these temporary pleasures as having an inner nature of pleasure. If sitting down really had an inner nature of comfort, then the longer we sat, the more comfortable we should feel. Instead, what was at first pleasant becomes painful. Can you think of a pleasurable experience that, if overindulged, does *not* turn into pain? When we begin to partake of our usual pleasures like eating, drinking, or making pleasant conversation, they seem enjoyable and satisfying, but if we keep engaging in them continuously, they become annoying, or downright painful. In the end, ordinary pleasurable feelings fade; they are unstable. As Aryadeva says in his text *Four Hundred Stanzas:*

> Pleasure, when prolonged,
> Is seen to change into pain.
> Pain, when prolonged,
> Does not likewise change into pleasure.

So, if you think about it, you can see that ordinary pleasures have an underlying nature of misery; this means you should not be satisfied with them.

3. *The suffering of pervasive conditioning.* This refers to the fact that our minds and bodies operate under the influence of destructive emotions such as lust and hatred, and under the influence of actions (karma) such as stealing and murder driven by those destructive emotions. Even neutral states of feeling (neither pleasure nor pain) are under the influence of causes and conditions beyond our control. This is the root of all levels of pain. As the great sage Tsongkhapa says:

In the same way that someone bearing a heavy burden cannot be happy as long as the burden must be borne, you too will suffer as long as you carry the burden of a mind-body complex appropriated through afflictive emotions and karmas driven by them. Though you have occasional moments when painful feeling is absent, because the mind-body complex is firmly embedded in the dysfunctional tendencies of suffering and afflictive emotions, the suffering of pervasive conditioning is still present, and therefore myriad sufferings are just on the verge of arising in countless ways. Since the suffering of such conditionality pervades all pain and is the root of the other two types of suffering, meditate on it often in order to become disenchanted with it.

Practitioners on the first rung of capacity seek to avoid the worst physical and mental pains of transmigrations as animals, hungry ghosts, and hell-beings by attaining high status within cyclic existence as humans or gods. On the next rung, practitioners of middling capacity seek to overcome all three levels of suffering by attaining liberation from all the various forms of cyclic existence, getting beyond even the suffering of life driven by afflictive emotions. On the final rung, practitioners of great capacity seek to overcome the problem of the predispositions left in the mind by those destructive emotions, which prevent them from the full perfection of altruistic omniscience and thus limit their attempts to help others; their aim is not just liberation from cyclic existence but the final attainment of the great enlightenment of Buddhahood.

In this way, Atisha showed how the many modes of Buddhist

practice are all included in the practices of three levels of gradually increasing capacity—lesser, middling, and great. The earlier practices are necessary prerequisites to advance to the higher outlook. As the Indian master Shura says:

> A person of great capacity should practice all these; they are branches of the path of the supreme intention to be free.

All of these are required to achieve what you yourself need to attain: the perfection of knowledge that Shakyamuni Buddha himself attained. Since we seek Buddhahood in order to be of greatest service to others, we must identify what is needed to achieve it—an altruistic intention to become enlightened, strong enough to cherish others more than yourself. Therefore, all Buddha's teachings are either directly or indirectly concerned with engendering this altruistic attitude, and increasing its force: they feed into it.

The Buddhist practices directly involved with generating this altruism are included in the cycle of teachings for beings of great capacity. However, in order to develop great compassion for the suffering of others, it is necessary to identify its main form, which is the suffering from pervasive conditioning. It is easiest to identify in yourself, so prior to developing great compassion you must develop your own intention to get out of the cyclic round of suffering. As Shantideva's *A Guide to the Bodhisattva's Way of Life* says:

> How could those who even for their own welfare
> Have not previously even in a dream
> Dreamed of such an attitude
> Engender it for others' sake?

Seeking your own relief from cyclic existence is included in the teachings for persons of medium capacity, who work on turning away from all forms of cyclic existence, going beyond the beginner's emphasis on solely achieving happy rebirths within cyclic existence. Prior to doing that, we must undermine our excessive attachment to the superficial appearances of this lifetime; the techniques for accomplishing this are included in the cycle of teachings for persons of lesser capacity.

As you can see, each of these practices is a stepping-stone for the development of the next perspective. So why are all of these not just included in the one category for the achievement of great capacity? If this were the case, practitioners might proudly think from the start that they were already on a high level, whereas with practices in three distinct categories, practitioners can realistically identify their own present level. In addition, those who for the moment do not aspire to high levels of practice can find what they need, since each level is presented in terms of what is to be accomplished, why we need to achieve it, and the techniques needed to practice it.

Atisha's *Lamp for the Path to Enlightenment* provides in complete form all levels of practice as we advance toward achieving full enlightenment. Since this text contains the full array of practices found in Buddha's teachings, all of the major sects of Tibetan Buddhism have taken on the task of perpetuating Atisha's teaching with basically similar presentations of the path.

TYPES OF TEACHINGS

When a fully qualified guru or lama offers guidance to a qualified student that is directly appropriate to that person's situation, there is no need for the student to study many texts. Having received from the lama express instructions for removing obstacles and gaining advancement, the student concentrates on meditation. The lama gives guidance appropriate to the student's changing needs as he or she progresses. There are other cases in which a lama who has reached a high level of spiritual development expresses his or her realizations for appropriate students in the form of spiritual songs, such as those by Indian yogis like Saraha and by lamas in all of the Tibetan sects.

Another type of Buddhist teaching is found in the comprehensive writings by great scholars such as the famed seventeen pandits of Nalanda. These core teachings include Nagarjuna's *Collections of Reasonings,* Maitreya's *Five Doctrines,* Asanga's *Five Treatises,* Shantideva's *A Guide to the Bodhisattva's Way of Life,* and so on. Thus, there are two types of teachings: those taught privately for particular students and those that present a comprehensive approach. Presentations of the stages of the path by Atisha and Tibetan authors such as Tsongkhapa are comprehensive teachings, based on the procedure of the Nalanda tradition.

When teachings aimed at particular students are examined as a body of work, it is possible for their surface or literal meanings not to be in agreement, since their purpose is to help in ways appropriate to a student's current situation. Buddha himself sometimes taught this way, based on a trainee's need. When these teachings are compared with comprehensive teachings, the latter are more important. From the perspective of the great general texts you can understand the thought behind those teachings given to particular students.

The more you become acquainted with the vast scope of the great texts, the less likely you will be to take a wrong turn in your understanding. This is because there is danger in just latching on to the literal meaning of a particular passage without placing it in context. With this in mind, Tsongkhapa says at the beginning of his *Great Treatise on the Stages of the Path:*

> Nowadays those making effort at yoga have studied little,
> And those who have studied much are not skilled in the
>   essential points of practice.
> Viewing the scriptures with partial sight, most are unable
> To discriminate the meaning of the scriptures with reasoning.

In my own experience I have found great benefit from looking into and practicing a wide variety of Buddhist teachings.

PRACTICALITY IS IMPORTANT

To practice you need to study, but when you study you need to be able to distill the practical essence of the text. Though you might know all about a wide range of topics, if you do not know how to bring these together in actual implementation, your mind will function as if fractured into many pieces.

Before writing the *Great Treatise on the Stages of the Path,* Tsongkhapa himself received all three lineages of transmission of Atisha's *Lamp for the Path to Enlightenment:* one in connection with the great texts, another not so vast but still associated with the great texts, and then a more condensed version with essential instructions for particular students. The school to which all three belong is called "Word As Guiding-Advice" (Kadam), because it takes all of the Buddha's words as advice for implementation in spiritual practice for a single individual. As the great Tibetan yogi Jangchup

Rinchen said, "Understand all scriptures as instructions for practice."

From this perspective you can immediately understand how practices described in other texts fit into the framework of the path to enlightenment. This broad view of the levels of practice will keep you from becoming biased, from looking down on a text because, for instance, it does not teach the highest levels of the path. You will understand that all of the practices are needed for a person to achieve Buddhahood, some early in the path and some later. Because these practices are arranged beginning at the level of a very troubled mind and extending through gradual training to greater and greater levels of peacefulness, when you read Buddha's word or its commentaries, you can easily understand what practices are aimed at achieving temporarily favorable lives within the round of birth and death, which ones are aimed at achieving liberation from cyclic existence, and which ones are aimed at achieving the altruistic omniscience of Buddhahood.

Not having this broad outlook, some people in countries where Buddhism had spread claimed that certain texts were not spoken by the Buddha, which claim put those who accepted those texts in a position of having to prove that Buddha did indeed speak them; this made for a lot of controversy and quarrelling back and forth. Similar bias can be seen in sects of Tibetan Buddhism claiming that certain teachings are sufficient and others are of no use. (I imagine this occurs in sects in other countries, too.) This is what happens when you do not view the entire range of scriptures as guidance or advice, and therefore not contradictory. We always need to be wary of destructive emotions, such as desire to elevate ourselves above others; they are very powerful, ready to corrupt even the most religious endeavors.

You may be thinking that because the great texts set forth doctrines that are not applicable to your daily practice at your present level, you need to seek advice somewhere else. It might look to you as if the great texts provide philosophical explanations merely for debate with others, and other shorter texts provide what is to be practiced. This is a great mistake. You need to understand that all of the Buddha's scriptures and their commentaries are necessary for your enlightenment, and you need to know how to take all of them as guidance for implementation in practice, now or later. It would be ridiculous to study one thing and then practice something else. At a minimum the higher teachings provide a map for future spiritual progress that itself will influence your journey.

RUNGS OF PRACTICE

In the stages of the path to enlightenment, the lower levels of the path provide foundations for developing a broad attitude of caring for a vast number of sentient beings. Therefore, even though Buddha taught certain students, based on their mental outlook, that they should seek peace and happiness for themselves alone, and hence prohibited them from engaging in many activities and many purposes, these limited teachings are not the focus of the stages of the path to enlightenment. Indeed, in terms of yourself you need few activities and few purposes, but in terms of the well-being of others you need many. This is the outlook of altruism called the Bodhisattva attitude. In fact, if you conduct too few activities for the sake of sentient beings, it is an infraction of the Buddhist vow that calls for maintaining that altruistic attitude.

I cannot help but observe that we often are content with merely wishing and praying for the happiness of others, whereas for our own purposes we do everything we can for our betterment, not just wishing!

STARTING OUT

Now let us turn to discussing the three levels in greater detail. To this end I will be drawing from Tsongkhapa's *Great Treatise on the Stages of the Path* as well as his *Medium-Length Exposition of the Stages of the Path*. Tsongkhapa was a great scholar; there are eighteen volumes of his collected works, and although that number is not extremely large compared to some other Tibetans, his works are of extremely high quality. His explanations of the great texts, while concise, are also amazingly insightful. He focuses on the difficult points, citing in his explanation of the wisdom of emptiness, for instance, the passages in Indian commentaries that are the hardest to understand. In his *The Essence of Eloquence*, when he explains the Mind-Only view he focuses on the Chapter on Reality in Asanga's *Grounds of Bodhisattvas*, which, while being a tiny portion of that very long text, contains many abstruse passages. These are either not understood well or raise doubt, so he emphasizes them. His level of scholarship is indeed extraordinary.

When you look into Tsongkhapa's writings, those later in his life reveal the experiences he gained by implementing key teachings, showing clearly that he had achieved high levels of realizations. In terms of both scriptural scholarship and practical realizations he was highly developed—both a great scholar and an accomplished adept. Those later writings also show his integrity, when he takes stances different from and even contrary to those in his early writings. He resists the temptations of pretension and stubbornness.

INITIAL LEVEL OF PRACTICE

7

Recognizing Our
Fortunate Situation

Why would I waste this attainment of such a good life!
When I act as though it is insignificant, I deceive myself.
What could be more foolish than this!

—TSONGKHAPA

Our age is called the Era of the Lamp because in this time a thousand Buddhas will illuminate the wisdom that realizes selflessness, which is the antidote to all destructive emotions. Buddhist texts call our world the "tolerable world," since we have access to the antidote to mistaking the nature of self, and therefore have no need to fear afflictive emotions; this allows us to tolerate being in such a bad state.

Without that antidote, destructive emotions would be all-powerful. Not recognizing the mistake of exaggerating self, we even take refuge in this attitude, allowing it to rest in the center of our hearts, thinking "I," "I," "I," "I" incessantly, valuing such a self highly. Due to this, afflictive emotions control us, forcing us to come under the influence of a host of counterproductive attitudes. However, by seeking out the teaching of selflessness we can generate wisdom that permits us to see this misapprehension for what it really is, allowing us to overcome ignorance.

Consider the fortunate situation we are presently in. We are free from major conditions that would prevent religious practice, and we have many favorable endowments. First, if we had been born into any of the transmigrations lower than a human, we would not have an opportunity to practice. We would not even think to engage in transformative practice, never mind be able to find someone teaching it. As an animal, for instance, we would be unable to meditate on impermanence, selflessness, or an altruistic intention to become enlightened, and unable to cultivate unlimited love and compassion. Though we could have love and compassion mixed with desire and hatred, anything beyond that would be impossible. This is why we need to value the fact that we have been born with a human body.

Let me tell you a joke. Once there was a lama in Tibet who, while teaching, spoke about how rare it is to attain a human birth. There was a Chinese person in the audience who turned to the person next to him and said, "It seems he never went to China!"

Indeed, merely to be born as a human is not in itself so amazing. If we had been born human in a dark age before a Buddha or a similar religious teacher had appeared, we could not have encountered their teachings; so it is decidedly to our advantage that this is not the case. We have been born during the Era of the Lamp when a thousand Buddhas will appear and at a time when Shakyamuni Buddha's teaching has already spread widely in the world. That makes us extremely fortunate.

Also, if we lacked the full complement of senses, practice would be difficult. Blind, we could not read texts; deaf, we could not hear lectures. If we were extremely dull, reflective thinking would be difficult. But we were not born that way; we have sufficient faculties for religious practice, which is very fortunate. And if you are reading these words, I assume you have an interest in religious practice. This situation is truly wonderful.

RARENESS OF THIS OPPORTUNITY

> One who is born as a human
> And then becomes involved in ill-deeds
> Is even more foolish than one who fills with vomit
> A gold vessel adorned with jewels.
>
> —Nagarjuna's *Letter*
> *to a Friend*

If endowment as a human could be attained again and again over the course of lifetimes, it would not be so bad if we did not use it and wasted it. However, life as a human is rare. Why? All impermanent phenomena are dependent upon causes and conditions, and this human physical life-support system that is potentially so effective requires high-quality causes. What are these causes? A human lifetime requires pure moral activity in a former life. Beyond this, a human lifetime during which transformative practice can be achieved requires prior engagement in virtues such as charity and patience, and these virtuous acts themselves need to be consciously aimed toward attaining the time and qualities needed for religious practice. With this motivation these acts will not be wasted by having their karmic results take place in a lifetime as a smart animal, for instance.

Thus three factors are needed to become a highly endowed human: fundamental moral behavior, practicing generosity and the like, and dedication of these practices toward bearing fruition in a human lifetime. If we consider whether we ourselves now have in place the causes and conditions to ensure a favorable rebirth like the one we have now, we see that most of us—even if we know something about spiritual endeavor and believe in its effectiveness—are still so conditioned in our destructive emotions that we are drawn into nonvirtuous actions as if by nature. And even when we think to perform virtuous actions, we seldom produce anything of high quality.

Why? The power of a deed, virtuous or nonvirtuous, depends on preparation, execution, and completing it. For instance, a powerful virtuous action such as meditation requires good motivation in its preparatory phase, high-quality enactment during the meditation itself, taking joy in the activity, and dedicating its force to altruistic enlightenment at its conclusion, without regrets. The same is true for a nonvirtuous action: whether it is a deed of murder, theft, lying, or the like, the motivation is an afflictive emotion, and if the act is performed with eagerness and without shame and if at the end you have a sense of satisfaction, the nonvirtuous deed becomes particularly powerful as a negative force.

If these factors are weak, the result is weak. Indeed, it is difficult when meditating, for instance, to maintain a strong motivation—the intention to extricate yourself from cyclic existence as well as to generate love, compassion, and an altruistic intention to become enlightened. It is also difficult to conduct the various steps of the actual meditation mindfully and without distraction.

In addition, strong anger, whenever it occurs, can undermine the effects of a virtuous action. Fortunately, the bad effects of a nonvirtuous action can be mitigated, in four ways: by disclosing it, by regretting having done it, by intending not to do it in the future, and by engaging in virtuous actions, such as public service. Whereas we seem to effortlessly generate irritation and anger, these virtuous actions of disclosure, contrition, reformed intention, and counteractive acts usually come from hard conscious effort.

When we consider the impediments to ensuring a favorable lifetime next time around, we see that it is difficult to attain the state of being true practitioners in body, speech, and mind. In this light, it becomes very clear that this precious human life-support system that we already have achieved is difficult to gain and therefore should be used wisely.

THE NEED TO PRACTICE NOW

Since this body of complete leisure and opportunity
Was very difficult to get, and once obtained
Will be very difficult to have again,
Make it meaningful by striving at practice.

—ATISHA

Appreciate how rare and full of potential your situation is in this world, take joy in it, and use it to your best advantage. In this context you can put your analytical intelligence to work diminishing the causes of suffering—the three poisons of lust, hatred, and ignorance. Gradually, over time, you can get rid of destructive emotions altogether, and can train in altruistic attitudes and deeds. As the Indian scholar-yogi Shura said:

Human life is a stream of good qualities better than a wish-granting jewel. Having attained it, who would waste it?

Everyone wants happiness and does not want suffering, and happiness and suffering depend on virtue and nonvirtue, respectively. Destructive emotions make the mind untamed and unhappy; to the degree that these counterproductive emotions diminish, the mind is happier, more at ease. Hence the key to happiness is whether the mind is tamed. This means that taming the mind is a transformative practice. I look at it this way:

In this world there are more than six billion humans, each of whom wants happiness, not suffering. Among them, there are three groups: those who accept transformative practice, those who deny its value and avoid it, and those who neither accept nor reject it. Which people are happier, those who accept it, or those who reject it? It seems to me that those who reject transformative practice generally do not see destructive emotions as problematic; rather than viewing lust and hatred as toxic, they allow themselves to get roiled by these attitudes. Those who accept transformative practice, and Buddhism in particular, view lust and hatred as emotions to be avoided, so for the most part they are more peaceful.

This is why it is necessary to practice. Given that we are currently endowed with the extraordinary qualities that enable us to practice, we must do so right now, for there is no guarantee that we will have such a situation in a future life. As Tsongkhapa says:

You should think, "Day and night I will make good use of this body of mine, which is a home of illness, a basis for the sufferings of old age, and lacks a core like a bubble."

USING THIS LIFE INTELLIGENTLY

As we have seen, Buddhist doctrines and practices call for analytical reflection. Fortunately, as humans we have a tremendous capacity for thought. Assisted by powerful analysis, we can generate altruism that is immeasurable in scope.

In order to develop an altruistic intention to become enlightened we must first identify enlightenment itself. We do this by understanding that the minds of all sentient beings are empty of inherent existence, which leads to an awareness that the very concept of inherent existence itself is mistaken. The basic nature of sentient beings is the capacity for enlightenment, which we call Buddha-nature.

To understand that all sentient beings possess the foundation for becoming enlightened, you need analytical wisdom. First you need to understand that all of your problems stem from your mind's mistaken view of yourself, of other people, and of all things as existing in and of themselves. When you see that this is a mistake, you realize that you can become enlightened, after which you can extend this realization to all sentient beings; they too can become enlightened. This lays the groundwork for developing the desire to help everyone toward enlightenment.

Without analytical wisdom, altruism cannot be achieved. Without it, you are caught in the sway of continuous distraction. With it, you can engender a strong aspiration to help others by achieving your own enlightenment. With it, you can realize that phenomena seem to exist solidly in and of themselves but do not. This is why great Buddhist adepts over the ages have emphasized that the human life we have already attained is so meaningful.

With wisdom we can attain high spiritual development. When

you consider that on this basis beings such as Nagarjuna attained great progress, you will see that there is no reason why you cannot attain the same. This encouragement is crucial.

Contemplation

Consider:

1. Presently you have a very fortunate situation, for you are free from obstacles to religious practice, and you possess many favorable attributes that enable you to achieve high spiritual development.

2. This situation is rare.

3. Attaining such a situation in the next lifetime requires fundamentally moral behavior, practicing generosity and so forth, and aiming their effects toward being reborn in a well-endowed human lifetime.

4. The bad effects of a nonvirtuous action can be mitigated in four ways: by disclosing it, by regretting having done it, by intending not to do it in the future, and by engaging in virtuous actions such as public service.

5. Virtuous deeds should be performed by preparing a good motivation in advance, with high-quality execution, and by dedicating its force to altruistic enlightenment at its conclusion, without regrets.

6. It is important to develop a distaste for destructive emotions.

7. Think to yourself: *Day and night I will make good use of this body of mine, which is a home of illness and the basis for the sufferings of old age, and lacks a core like a bubble.*

8

Knowing You Will Die

A place to live unharmed by death
Does not exist.
Not in space, not in the sea,
Nor if you stay in the midst of mountains.
—BUDDHA

In order to counteract the mistaken notion that this life is permanent, Buddha taught meditation on death. The main reasons for his doing so can be understood by considering what happens when you are not mindful of death. Most of the people in this world who are stirring up trouble, ruining their lives and those of others, have a strong and mistaken sense of their own permanence. Believing that they, their relatives, and their friends will stay around for a long time, and thinking that their own happiness can be stable and permanent, they concentrate on promoting their own group at the expense of any other, and engage in many activities that bring ruin to others and themselves.

The assumption that we will be around for a long time, as if we were permanent, undermines both self and others by creating counterproductive ideas and endeavors. The responsibility for this rests solely on our mistaken view of permanence, on not being aware of death. If you remain aware that your own death can happen at any time, you will not fall into so much trouble. Mindful that your own death is inevitable, you will be drawn into thinking about whether there is a future life. Even if you only suspect that there is, you will take interest in the quality of that life, of what it might be like. This will lead you to think about karma—the cause and effect of actions—drawing you away from choosing activities of a harmful nature and encouraging you to engage in activities that are beneficial. This itself will lend your life a positive purpose.

In addition, if you avoid the mere mention of death as if it were off limits, then on the day when death comes, you may become frightened and uncomfortable. However, if you contemplate the fact that death is something that happens naturally, this can make a big difference. When you become familiar with death, you can make preparations for dying, and decide what you should do with your mind at that time. Then on that day your preparation will have its effect; you will think "Ah, death has come," and act as you planned, free from fright.

IMMINENCE OF DEATH

Now is the time to make ourselves
different from domesticated animals.
—THE GREAT TIBETAN YOGI
JANGCHUP RINCHEN

Meditation on the imminence of death takes place by way of three root reflections, each of which is based on three reasons, leading to a decision. Here is a summary, followed by a step-by-step explanation.

First root: Contemplation that death is definite

1. because death cannot be avoided
2. because our life span cannot be extended and grows ever shorter
3. because even when we are alive there is little time to practice.

FIRST DECISION: I MUST PRACTICE.

Second root: Contemplation that the time of death is uncertain

4. because our life span in this world is indefinite
5. because the causes of death are many and the causes of life are few
6. because the time of death is unknowable due to the fragility of the body.

SECOND DECISION: I MUST PRACTICE NOW

Third root: Contemplation that at the time of death nothing helps except transformative practice

7. because at the time of death our friends are no help
8. because at the time of death our wealth is no help
9. because at the time of death our body is no help.

THIRD DECISION: I WILL PRACTICE NONATTACHMENT
TO ALL OF THE WONDERFUL THINGS OF THIS LIFE

Death Is Definite

Once something is produced, whether it is an object in the external world or a being living in it, it gradually moves toward destruction. According to some cosmologists, it has been twenty-five billion years since the big bang, the cataclysmic explosion that gave birth to our universe; others say twelve billion, while still others posit seventeen or eighteen. In any case, there was a beginning to this universe, and thus it is certain that at some point it will come to an end. Even mountains that have been here for millions of years are eroding moment by moment, so, similarly, the beings living in this world, who are far more fragile than mountains, are inexorably moving toward death moment by moment.

Our bodies rely on a set of conditions so complicated that even a small deviation can create a problem. If our bodies were just filled with fluid, that would be one thing, but the human body is extremely complex; each of our five major organs—heart, lungs, liver, spleen, and kidneys—depends on its respective system, which, if thrown out of balance, can cause problems. Relative to solid objects, our bodies are fragile and require continuous maintenance.

Though humans have existed in this world for around a million years, no one has successfully avoided the fate of death, and neither will we. Death is definite. As Buddha said:

> The varieties of lives in the world are impermanent like
>   autumn clouds.
> The birth and death of beings are like watching a dance.
> The passage of life is like lightning in the sky.
> It moves quickly, like a waterfall.

The certainty of dying calls us to engage in spiritual practice.

The Time of Death Is Uncertain

We all know in the back of our minds that we will die, but we keep thinking that this will not happen for a long time. Right until the moment we actually die, we think that it will not happen for quite a while yet. This attitude causes us to put off achieving the great aim of real lasting happiness.

Since the illusion of permanence fosters procrastination, it is crucial to reflect repeatedly on the fact that death could come at any time. Our lives are fragile, and even things that usually sustain life, such as medicine and cars, can turn into causes of death. As Nagarjuna says in his *Precious Garland of Advice*:

> You are living amidst the causes of death
> Like a lamp standing in a strong breeze.

The fragility of life calls us to make a decision to implement spiritual practice right now. Religion is not physical. Although both physical and verbal virtuous actions are important, religion is matter of mental transformation. This means not just understanding something new but suffusing your mental continuum with this knowledge in order to tame your unruly mind and put it in service of virtue. This means that you must practice now. If you do whatever you can at the present juncture to transform your mind, then even sickness and pain while you are dying will not disturb the strong sense of peace, firm like a mountain, deep in your mind.

At Death Nothing Helps Except Having Practiced

Successful practice is essential. If we consider how we usually spend our days, most of us practice just a little, muttering a few mantras, and if we are at ease, we think a little bit about "all sentient beings," but if we get the least bit stirred up, we fight with others, deceive them, and lose sight of our spiritual aspirations. This sort of sporadic activity is not real practice, for it is unable to influence more intense situations. By overemphasizing our own temporary comfort, we lose sight of the long-term goal.

In Lhasa, the capital of Tibet, a person who was walking along came upon a fellow who was sitting in meditation. He asked the fellow, "What are you doing?" "I am meditating patience," was the response. So the man said, "Then eat shit!" The meditator lashed back, "*You* eat shit!" The meditator could not even withstand a little teasing.

When things are going well, it is easy to take on the outward appearance of calm through meditation, but the slightest ruffle in the environment exposes how superficial our attempts are. If, while we are still alive, our practice is not effective at times of need, then it will be difficult for it to have much effect at the time of death. This is why it is necessary to practice in such a way that you are profoundly affected.

Put persistent effort over months and years into actually affecting your outlook, perspective, and attitudes. In time you will find that although your body is essentially the same, your mind has undergone profound change. After this transformation, no matter what unfavorable circumstances arise, these events will serve to build character, advance your spiritual practice, and accelerate your progress toward enlightenment. At this point, you are a real practitioner.

The two essential spiritual practices are altruism and the view of emptiness, or dependent-arising. When you come to experience them to some degree, these perspectives will be loyal friends and unwavering protectors. These attitudes help from the present moment right through death, so make these practices the root and essence of your life. This requires making a decision to give up attachment to things that are actually superficial and fleeting. Not coming under the influence of procrastination but practicing as well as you can: this is the way.

CLEARING UP MISTAKEN NOTIONS

In 1954 I traveled to Beijing to meet with Mao Zedong. During our final meeting in 1955 he told me, "Religion is poison for two reasons. The first is that it harms development of the nation. The second is that it diminishes the population." His thought was that when many people become monastic, this will reduce the number of births. In hindsight we can say now that more monastics is just what China needed to reduce overpopulation! Mao simply did not understand what religion means.

Sometimes when people come to accept that they might die at any time, they draw the mistaken conclusion that planning for this life is useless, so they do not really accomplish anything. However, this is not the point; we just need to place less emphasis on merely our own happiness, on living a long time, accumulating more and more wealth, building a house beyond what we really need, and the like. Instead we need to engage in activities for the welfare of the society as a whole, such as building schools, hospitals, and factories; we need to base our lives on altruistic concern.

Consider, for example, what Atisha's Tibetan student, Dromton, did in the eleventh century. Though he had realized the full scope of practices for becoming enlightened, he built a temple at Rato in central Tibet; he did not just sit around thinking, "Oh my, I might die today." Similarly, at the beginning of the fifteenth century, Tsongkhapa not only built Ganden Monastic University, but once it had been built, he advised his student Jamyang Chojay to build a similar institution of learning near Lhasa called Drepung, and advised another student, Jamchen Chojay, to build another on the other side of Lhasa, called Sera. They all undertook large projects to advance the welfare of society for hundreds and even thousands of years.

Similarly, the First Dalai Lama, Gendun Drup, was both a highly learned scholar and an accomplished adept, a true Bodhisattva. He decided to build a monastic university called Trashi Lhunpo in western Tibet. Early in the morning he would lecture on important texts, and then he assigned his various students to visit individuals in that area to collect donations to build the monastery. He himself directed the construction workers. He was fully involved in everything—teaching, writing books, collecting donations, and building. He made these efforts not for his private welfare but for the good of society; he was a simple monk and owned nothing, but he engaged in many activities for the long-term welfare of others.

We, on the other hand, are often small-minded. When asked to do something for society, we pull back, citing lack of time, or impermanence, but when it comes to our own welfare, whether it involves more money, a better place to live, or the like, we forget about impermanence. We all need to be wary of this, examining our lives to see if this is what we are doing.

ADVICE FOR THE DAY OF DEATH

All of us are going to die, so we need to consider the type of attitude we will have as we are dying. If during the course of your life you have become accustomed to virtuous attitudes, then through that force of familiarization you will be able to produce a virtuous attitude while dying. You can help to recall this attitude by setting up a religious image near your bed, or by being reminded by a friend. If, however, you have accumulated many nonvirtues during the course of your life, it is crucial near the end to develop a strong sense of contrition for what you have done. This makes it more likely that you will be reborn in a favorable life.

Conversely, if despite having engaged in many virtuous endeavors during your life, near the time of death you develop strong lust or hatred, there is danger that this will adversely influence your rebirth. You should take care of your attitude at that time, seeking to die with mental calmness within an attitude of compassion, love, faith, or other virtuous outlook. When someone you know is dying, be careful not to disturb the person by provoking desire or anger.

Contemplation

Consider:

1. The illusion of permanence, or being unaware of death, creates the counterproductive idea that you will be around for a long time; this, in turn, leads to superficial activities that undermine both yourself and others.
2. Awareness of death draws you into thinking about whether there is a future life and taking interest in the quality of that life, which promotes helpful long-term activities and diminishes dedication to the merely superficial.
3. To appreciate the imminence of death, think deeply about the implications of the three roots, nine reasons, and three decisions:

   First root: Contemplation that death is definite
   1. because death cannot be avoided

2. because our life span cannot be extended and grows ever shorter

3. because even when we are alive there is little time to practice.

FIRST DECISION: I MUST PRACTICE.

Second root: Contemplation that the time of death is uncertain

4. because our life span in this world is indefinite

5. because the causes of death are many and the causes of life are few

6. because the time of death is unknowable due to the fragility of the body.

SECOND DECISION: I MUST PRACTICE NOW.

Third root: Contemplation that at the time of death nothing helps except transformative practice

7. because at the time of death our friends are no help

8. because at the time of death our wealth is no help

9. because at the time of death our body is no help.

THIRD DECISION: I WILL PRACTICE NONATTACHMENT TO ALL OF THE WONDERFUL THINGS OF THIS LIFE.

4. Make sure not to develop strong lust or hatred near your time of death, since this could adversely influence your rebirth.

5. If you have engaged in many nonvirtues during your life, it is important near the end to develop strong contrition for what you have done; this will help your next life.

9

Thinking About Future Lives

If there is no limit
To this ocean of suffering,
O childish one, why are you,
While sunk in it, not concerned?

—ARYADEVA,

FOUR HUNDRED STANZAS

We all have to die, for this begins the process leading to the next life. You need to think about what it will be like after you die. If dying was like the drying up of a tree or a flower, it would not matter, but it is not like that. If you really think about what it will be like after death, you will take care to act in ways that will favorably affect your next rebirth.

You need to contemplate both that you must die and what it will be like in the next life. When you have done so, you will pay more attention to the deeper aspects of life; you will focus on the ways that karma works—the ways your own actions bring about specific effects. When you recognize that there is a future life, you will determine what is important, and with a corner of your mind you will start making preparations for that time.

WHAT HAPPENS AFTER DEATH?

When we consider what happens after death, we run into a lot of complications. For thousands of years people have wondered whether there is a future life or not. Some believe that consciousness arises in dependence upon the body, and thus when the body dies, the continuum of consciousness also comes to an end. Others believe that the mind or soul makes its way to a heaven or a hell. Still others, in certain non-Buddhist systems in India, for example, hold that the self is independent of the mind-body complex, which it discards to take on a new body in rebirth.

Buddhists assert that the self always has been reborn and is set up in dependence upon the mind-body complex for a given lifetime. This self, person, or "I" is mainly based on an individual continuum of consciousness. A particular human being is set up, or designated, in dependence upon a human mind-body complex, the core of which is a human continuum of consciousness.

Does this consciousness arise from the neurons of the brain or from something else? If it could be established with certainty that consciousness arises from the brain, it would be difficult to assert the existence of former and future lives. However, since there are people whose memories from former lives have been verified, we must take this into account somehow. Scientists should look into this topic; even if they start now, they will likely have to continue investigating into the twenty-second century!

In any case, based on our own experience we can clearly see that many types of consciousness arise in dependence upon physical organs such as the brain. For instance, it is obvious that sensory consciousness relies upon our eyes, ears, nose, tongue, and body. Buddhist texts themselves say that sense organs create the conditions for sensory consciousness by providing the receptors for colors and shapes, sounds, odors, tastes, and textures such as smoothness.

Just as material things such as our bodies depend upon their own causes and conditions, so consciousness itself depends upon its respective causes and conditions, which means there has to be a continuum of causes for its own type of entity. The particles of the body stem from genetic material provided by the parents, sperm and egg, which themselves stem from material provided by their parents, on back to simpler organisms, the earliest of which date back about a billion years ago. The causal continuum of our bodies can be traced back even further to the subtle material particles at the formation of this world system. Prior to that, Buddhist texts speak of very subtle material, particles of space, which are mentioned in the *Kalachakra Tantra* and its associated literature. Our bodies are the result of this continuum of material particles.

In a similar way, the luminous and cognitive nature of our consciousness has to have its own stream of essential causes in order to come into existence. Mindless matter cannot become conscious, even though it can provide certain necessary conditions, such as sense organs (like eyes) and physical objects to view (such as a gray building).

Scientists have recently shown that changes in the brain result from changes in thought. Cultivation of compassion, for instance, which brings about great changes in the mind, has been seen to affect the workings of the brain. Consciousness is not a single entity; it is vast and variegated. There are many types of consciousness, and many levels of coarseness and subtlety. Some types of consciousness depend upon the brain, and some do not.

Children from the same parents can be quite different mentally despite having had similar upbringings and educations. Although some differences do come from the fact that the bodies of children from the same parents do not have exactly the same genetic material, it would be difficult to fully explain the vast variation between children of the same parents in this way. Physical factors do indeed influence clarity of mind, vastness of outlook, and intelligence, but they do not provide the complete picture.

Habits in former lives could also be involved; certain attitudes could carry over and later affect the continuation of mind. If this is the case, then consciousness from the initial moment in the mother's womb is affected by earlier predispositions, which means we need to consider that this initial moment may stem from the mental stream of a former lifetime. As the great Indian logician Dharmakirti said:

> Because the non-conscious cannot be the essential cause of consciousness,
> The beginninglessness of cyclic existence is established.

For me, the strongest evidence for rebirth comes from those who accurately recall former lifetimes. Such people confirm the existence of former lives by direct memory, so no further proof is needed. In our own generation there have been Tibetans who have remembered former lifetimes in clear detail. Also, I am aware of two Indian girls who remember the life immediately preceding this one, as well as a three-year old boy who remembers his former life with great clarity: he died in a car accident. Many such instances were investigated by the late professor Ian Stevenson of the University of Virginia, who found quite a few people whose stories could be validated, which he describes in several books. Perhaps you yourself have encountered children who have told such stories, which are usually ignored, especially by those who do not accept the concept of former lifetimes. I believe it can be helpful to look into the stories told by very young children.

It seems to me that the existence of former lives is not determined by whether the majority of people remember or not; rather, one person's valid memory indicates that such past lives are the case for all of us, whether or not we ourselves remember them. A few of my acquaintances, true practitioners, have very clear memories of former lives that have emerged from their practice of meditation.

With consciousness proceeding in a continuous stream, death is like changing clothes when the present body can no longer be maintained. But was there an initial birth that set this stream in motion? If so, there would have to have been an initial consciousness, which would have to have been produced from a mindless state. This is absurd, which is why Buddhists say there is no beginning to the round of rebirth.

THE ORIGIN OF OUR WORLD SYSTEM

How did the galaxy itself form? If it was the result of the big bang, how did the big bang come about? We might feel that since impermanent causes need causes before them, it is best to posit an initial permanent cause, but the problem with this is still that the permanent lacks the capacity to produce impermanent effects because that would mean that something permanent led to change, which is impossible. Again, if we turn to a Creator God, it has to be asked whether it is permanent or impermanent, and we are left in the same quandary, since if a Creator God is impermanent, it has to be asked what its causes are. If it is another Creator God, then it too will need a Creator and on and on. Also, if a Creator God is posited as having a nature of infinite knowledge, sympathy, and power, that is problematic, given the often harrowing situations in the world.

Let me make it clear that I am not criticizing other religions; I am merely conveying the Buddhist perspective. My point is that Buddhism turns away from a permanent creator, and posits its own explanation. Just as a house is built by a person who is the builder, the entire world according to Buddhism is formed by the karmic influences of the beings who live in it. Our own former actions, called karmas, affect the formation of material particles that themselves are not made by karma; the karmas of beings living in the environment create conditions that gradually affect how it forms. Since our present world cannot have been formed after we took this present life, the karmas that shape our world must be from past lifetimes, even over a long course of time.

It seems to me that even if this perspective does not fulfill all of our questions, it is food for thought.

HOW KARMA SHAPES OUR LIVES

Just as the world itself is shaped by the karma of the beings who will inhabit it, certain of your own actions in this and previous lives determine how you will be reborn. All of us are born with a natural tendency to avoid physical and mental pain. So how is it that nevertheless we are drawn into situations of pain? It is because we do not accurately assess what produces suffering. Though we do not want pain, we do not know enough about what causes this effect because we do not pay sufficient attention to it. Sometimes we even cultivate the causes of pain: for the sake of temporary profit, people cheat others, or slaughter many animals out of desire for delicious food, or commit murder. Consider how much theft, sexual misconduct, lying, backbiting, harsh speech, and senseless gossip there is. These behaviors exemplify the fact that even though no one wants outright pain, by not paying any attention to what causes it we enthusiastically rush into actions that bring it on— sometimes to the point where it is irreversible.

In order to view those actions as faulty and to come to a strong determination to restrain them, we must reflect on the relationship between our actions and their fruits. By understanding the danger posed by certain actions we can turn away from those deeds. This is why Buddhist texts speak about the suffering that comes from unfavorable rebirths: to stimulate thought about what causes them.

TYPES OF REBIRTH

If you reflect on the suffering of beings in dire situations, such as many animals, and imagine yourself in a similarly vulnerable position, you will immediately see how difficult such a life is, and therefore how awful such a rebirth would be. The power of this realization will motivate you to refrain from such actions, or karmas, producing such a rebirth. (You cannot choose where you will be reborn, but your rebirth is driven by your own karma.)

Buddhist texts speak of three general categories of unfavorable births:

- animals who suffer from the strong killing the weak, from limited communication and ability to think, and from exploitation by humans;

- hungry ghosts who suffer from being unable to partake of food and drink because of their own physical deformities or because of harm in the environment;
- hell beings who mainly suffer from excessive heat and cold.

The situation of animals is obvious to us, as is the fact that many humans undergo sufferings similar to animals, hungry ghosts, and hell-beings.

To avoid taking rebirth in such dire situations and to attain rebirth in a more favorable situation we must engage in a moral practice that avoids the ten nonvirtues mentioned above:

- the three principal physical nonvirtues—killing, stealing, and sexual misconduct;
- the four principal verbal nonvirtues—lying, divisive talk, harsh speech, and senseless chatter;
- the three principal mental nonvirtues—covetousness, harmful intent, and wrong views.

To successfully avoid these, it is crucial to know the difference between good actions that create auspicious effects and bad actions that create negative effects. However, the more subtle relationships between particular virtuous actions in one life and exactly how they will reach fruition in a future life, are not evident to us. Although slightly obscure phenomena are accessible to us through analytical reasoning, such reasoning cannot penetrate extremely obscure topics. These effects of extremely obscure phenomena are known only to omniscient Buddhas; even highest level Bodhisattvas do not know these most subtle relationships. We have to rely on scripture while making sure that there is no contradiction within the Buddha's scriptures on a specific topic, either explicitly or implicitly, as well as no contradiction with effective reasoning or direct observation. This threefold examination of scripture is the means by which we can determine whether a scripture can be taken literally or requires interpretation.

Contemplation

Consider:

1. Material things such as your body depend upon various causes and conditions, which means there has to be a continuum of causes for such an entity. The material body stems from material provided by the parents, sperm and egg, which themselves stem from material provided by their parents, and so on.

2. Similarly, your consciousness depends upon its own causes and conditions, which points to a continuum of causes for the luminous and cognitive nature of your mind, which comes from former lives.

3. Also, given the vast range of differences between children of the same parents, it seems likely that cognitive predispositions from earlier lives are at work in this life.

4. Valid memory of previous lives confirms the existence of former lives. One person's valid memory indicates that such lives were experienced by all of us, whether or not we ourselves remember them.

5. There can be no beginning to the round of rebirth.

6. Just as a house is constructed by the builder, so the entire world that is our environment takes shape due to the karmic influences of the beings who live in the world, and from their past lifetimes over a long course of time.

7. Your own actions determine how you will be reborn, just as the world itself is shaped by the karmas of the beings who will inhabit it.

8. Reflect on the cause-and-effect relationship between actions and their fruits, understanding the implications.

9. Bring to mind the suffering of beings in a dire situation, including animals, and imagine yourself in a similarly exposed situation. This will inspire restraint from actions (karmas) producing a negative rebirth.

10. Work at avoiding the ten nonvirtues:

   • the three principal physical nonvirtues—killing, stealing, and sexual misconduct;

   • the four principal verbal nonvirtues—lying, divisive talk, harsh speech, and senseless chatter;

   • the three principal mental nonvirtues—covetousness, harmful intent, and wrong views.

10

Identifying the Refuge

Adrift in the bottomless ocean of cyclic existence,
Devoured by the fierce sea monsters
Of attachment and the like,
To whom should I go for refuge today?

— DIGNAGA

When we encounter unfavorable circumstances that our own techniques cannot overcome, we turn to a source of protection that we trust; we seek a refuge from situations that we ourselves cannot handle. For example, in a heavy rain we stay under a roof, and when cold we turn on heating as a protection against the cold; this is how we seek temporary help. As little children, our ultimate refuge is naturally our mother; our impulse to turn to her is so strong that later in life when a very frightening situation arises, we may even call out "Mother!"

The many religions of the world have developed a similar refuge in which they place their faith. Those that assert the existence of a creator God find their ultimate refuge in that God. Buddhists turn to three sources—known as the Three Jewels—in order to find ultimate refuge.

THE BUDDHIST REFUGE

To seek refuge we must first be alarmed by an undesired situation from which we seek relief. Here in this discussion about enlightenment our concern is with our own counterproductive emotions, which we recognize to be the troublemakers. We seek protection from them, and since what we are looking for is liberation from internal enemies, a temporary refuge is not sufficient.

In Buddhism, the refuge for those seeking release from counterproductive emotions is threefold: the Buddha who teaches the path to liberation; his teachings, which are the actual source of protection; and the spiritual community that helps us realize that refuge. We call these the Three Jewels, because like jewels they provide relief from the deprivations of cyclic existence.

Developing Conviction in the Sources of Refuge

If someone is turning to the Three Jewels for refuge, it is helpful to establish that omniscient Buddhahood exists. Even if we find the story of Shakyamuni Buddha's life in India more than 2,500 years ago to be full of amazement, it is not easy to gain conviction that he achieved mental and physical perfection. To do this a story is not sufficient; we need to establish that liberation from cyclic existence is possible. And to do that, it is necessary to establish that the means of achieving liberation are attainable; we need to gain conviction in the nonconceptual wisdom of deep meditation, and in the problem-free states that this wisdom brings about.

When you develop conviction in these paths and states that make liberation a reality, you will see that taking refuge in Buddha, his doctrine, and the spiritual community is a true possibility. Let me explain how such conviction could be gained.

As I have been saying from the beginning of this book, putting an end to our troubles rests on the doctrine of selflessness, the understanding of the emptiness of inherent existence. In his *Fundamental Treatise on the Middle Way,* Nagarjuna says:

> When afflictive emotions and actions cease, there is
> liberation.
> Afflictive emotions and actions arise from false conceptions.
> These arise from erroneous proliferations.
> Proliferations are ceased in emptiness.

The mistaken perception of inherent existence gives rise to mistaken thinking, which in turn generates the harmful emotions of lust, hatred, and so on. The force of those destructive emotions produces actions (karmas) infected by them, and these actions leave imprints in the mind that drive the painful round of repeated births. We can put an end to the proliferation of this ignorant misapprehension of oneself, others, and objects by cultivating the realization of emptiness. When this wisdom extinguishes all counterproductive emotions, we arrive at liberation from cyclic existence, the true resolution of all our problems.

Ignorance is the root cause of misery, causing spirals of counterproductive emotions and attendant troubles. As Nagarjuna's student Aryadeva puts it:

> Just as the sense of feeling pervades the body,
> Ignorance dwells in all afflictive emotions.

Therefore, all afflictive emotions are overcome
Through overcoming ignorance.

As mentioned earlier, "ignorance" here means not just the absence
of knowledge about how phenomena actually exist but also an
active misconception—seeing persons and things as if they exist
independently from their own side. This ignorance is uprooted
through the realization that all phenomena arise in dependence
upon other phenomena. Aryadeva continues:

When dependent-arising is seen,
Bewildering ignorance does not arise.
Therefore, with all endeavor here
I will set forth just discourse on this.

"Bewildering ignorance" mistakes dependence for independence.
Hence the antidote is to clearly see relationality, which we call
"dependent-arising."

When Nagarjuna says that the proliferating misconception
of inherent existence ceases in emptiness, what is emptiness? He
himself says it means dependent-arising:

We explain that dependent-arising
Is emptiness.
That itself means dependently set up.
This itself is the middle path.

Having identified that the true nature of things is that they are
empty, or dependently arisen, Nagarjuna continues:

Because there are no phenomena
That are not dependent-arisings,
There are no phenomena that are not
Empty of inherent existence.

This means that by seeing that all things are dependently arisen, and following the implications of this fact, you realize that phenomena are empty of inherent existence. Using the fact that phenomena are interdependent, you draw the conclusion that phenomena are not established in their own right. By dwelling on this thought over time, it will appear to your mind that this is really so.

Once you can establish through reasoning that phenomena do not exist as they appear to, which is solidly in their own right, you realize that your sense that people and objects exist in their own right exaggerates their status. Since your own experience shows you that interdependence is the way things are, you can decide that phenomena do not exist independently, gaining at least an inkling into the emptiness of inherent existence.

This is how thoughtful contemplation reveals the emptiness of inherent existence. A wise psychologist once told me that he had come to the conclusion that when we feel lust or hatred, 80 to 90 percent of our perception of the object of our emotions is an exaggeration; he came to this conclusion not from reflecting on Nagarjuna's statements but from his own analysis. This shows that through unbiased investigation you can come to understand how the mistaken assumption that phenomena exist independently in their own right serves as the basis of lust and hatred.

When you find yourself in the grip of strong afflictive emotions, examine whether that person or thing you lust after or hate so much actually exists as it appears. You will see that its appearance involves an exaggeration, and when you do, your destructive emotion built on this misperception will wilt, as if in embarrassment.

When you do not challenge appearances, but assent to them and consider a person or object to be entirely good or bad through and through, this causes you to desire it in all respects or to feel intense hatred for it. At those times you will make strong statements such as "He is awful!" "She is really terrible!" "He is terrific!" "She is fantastic!" However, when you begin to see that this extreme degree of true goodness or badness that seems to be intrinsic to the person simply does not exist, the emotion that is built on that exaggeration backs off, as if it sees the mistake we have made and pulls back.

Let me tell you a story. When my Senior Tutor Ling Rinpoche was still in Tibet before the Chinese invasion, he wanted a table lacquered, so he asked his attendant to take it to a Chinese artisan who was living in Lhasa. When his attendant arrived at the shop, the artisan was sitting with a broken antique teacup in his hand, staring at it and sighing. He told the attendant that earlier he had gotten angry and banged the cup down and broke it. Either he had been viewing the cup as 100 percent awful and smashed it down or he had been viewing a customer in his shop as 100 percent horrible and broke the cup to satisfy his anger. Now that his anger had subsided, he again saw the cup as a beautiful antique, and so he was still holding it in his hand, sighing. His warped perspective had melted away.

In situations like this you can clearly see that lust and hatred are based on going along with the appearance of qualities such as goodness or badness as if they truly, objectively exist in those persons or objects. This does not mean that good and bad, or favorable and unfavorable, do not exist, for they do, but it means that these qualities do not exist independently in the way that they appear to a lustful or a hateful mind.

Using this line of analysis, you can see that afflictive emotions are based on a mistaken conception, on ignorance of the way things truly are. As Aryadeva says:

Just as the sense of feeling pervades the body,
Ignorance dwells in all afflictive emotions.

Understand that lust and hatred are mistaken attitudes, and that their root, the ignorant conception that phenomena exist in their own right, independently, is also mistaken. It has no valid foundation. From this you will understand the wisdom of realizing that everything is a dependent-arising. As you cultivate this insight more and more, this realization will naturally become stronger and stronger, and you will find yourself less and less susceptible to feelings of lust and hatred.

This process shows how, through analysis, you can gradually bring about a change of attitude and, eventually, transformation of mind. Through this route you can develop conviction in what really can protect you, what really is a source of refuge. You can develop a sense, or inkling, that enlightenment is possible, because although physical attributes cannot be limitlessly developed simply because they depend on the body, mental qualities have a stable basis in the mind, which goes on continuously. If those mental qualities are founded in valid cognition, they can be developed into an unlimited state.

Four Authorities

According to the Sakya order of Tibetan Buddhism, Buddha's *valid scriptures* inspired *valid commentaries* on his words. Then, over the ages, those who practiced and came to fully realize the meaning of Buddha's word and the commentaries on it developed into *valid gurus* who taught those topics, and based on their explanations, trainees developed *valid experience.*

Although these four validities came into being in this order, for us to become certain of them we must first generate *valid experience*, at which point we will know that this beneficial experience stems from the teachings of *valid gurus* in whom we therefore gain true belief. Then knowing that the guru practices, for instance, Nagarjuna's *Fundamental Treatise on the Middle Way*, we come to view Nagarjuna's text as a *valid commentary*, and since that treatise derives from Buddha's teachings, we can gain conviction in *valid scriptures.* Thus in terms of our own confirmation of the four authorities, the sequence derives from valid experience.

It seems to me that there are two types of valid experience: higher and lower. Those on a high level of spiritual experience have, for example, trained in the altruistic intention to become enlightened to such a point that their wish to attain Buddhahood for the sake of others is genuine, without any contrivance; they also have realized emptiness with incontrovertible inference or even with direct perception; and they have developed meditative concentration to the point of becoming clairvoyant and generating miracles. We, however, being on a lower level, do not now have these qualities. Still, we could have a keen interest in the practice of love and compassion that effectively buoy our outlook when we become depressed or deflate us in situations when we become

proud. Even this lower level of attainment can be amazingly beneficial.

Similarly, even if we have not generated true realization of the
view of emptiness, reflection on dependent-arising and emptiness
engenders some insight, which is helpful in daily life. The same is
true for developing conviction in the cause and effect of karma.
For instance, when encountering a difficult circumstance in the
course of daily life, if you consider that it is an effect of former actions and must be faced, this will keep you from falling into a pit of
discouragement, of losing hope of being able to stand it. Or, if you
reflect on the suffering which stems from afflictive emotions, you
will see that once you fall under the influence of ignorance, there is
no way to completely avoid such problems. Whether you are facing
internal or external difficulties, you will think, "This is the nature
of cyclic existence," and you will not resort to counterproductive
drastic actions, such as suicide.

Once we can confirm that our own level of experience of altruism is truly helpful, we can also get a good idea of how amazingly beneficial it must be to develop altruism to the point where
it flows naturally. Similarly, once we confirm that even low-level
experience of dependent-arising and emptiness helps so much, we
can glimpse what might be possible at a higher level. Even with
this low level of *valid experience* we can determine that there are *valid
gurus*, which leads us to understand that there are *valid commentaries*
on Buddha's teachings, which are the *valid scriptures*. And based on
these four validities, we can gain a level of conviction in Buddhahood as a state that includes profound and vast mental and physical perfection.

This seems to me to be a good way to approach identifying the
objects of refuge—Buddha, his doctrine, and the spiritual commu-

nity. By reflecting on the truth of dependent-arising and emptiness, you can understand that there is such a thing as a pure state of mind, and you can glimpse the spiritual realizations that yield such a pure state (the realized doctrine). From this you understand that there are those who have attained levels that involve such realized purity (the spiritual community), as well as those who have brought this process of spiritual development to perfection (Buddhas). When this is clear to your mind, you will see the reasonableness of turning for refuge to the Buddha, his doctrine, and the spiritual community.

A Buddha's Compassion

Why is Shakyamuni Buddha valued so highly? By developing great compassion to an unbounded state, with sympathy for an infinite number of sentient beings that is like a mother's feeling for her own sweet child, he developed a boundless intention to help all beings overcome all obstacles to happiness, and worked eon after eon in order to be of the greatest benefit to others. At the culmination of his practice, he succeeded in attaining all realizations and removing all obstructions to his own enlightenment, solely for the sake of continuously assisting others to rise to the same state. This is why it is suitable to go to him for refuge.

As the sixth-century Indian scholar of Buddhist logic Dignaga says:

Homage to the one who has become authoritative,
Who has taken on the task of benefiting beings,
Teacher, One-Gone-to-Bliss, Protector.

The reason why Buddha is authoritative is that out of a desire to help others, he completed the training in compassion. Since an altruistic attitude alone is not sufficient, he became familiar with the wisdom that realizes selflessness, fulfilling the practices for overcoming obstacles and gaining complete realization, whereby he became an unparalleled, true protector of others.

Nagarjuna also speaks of compassion as the fundamental quality, and Chandrakirti says at the beginning of his *Introduction to the Middle Way*:

> Compassion itself is seen to be
> The seed of a rich harvest, water for growth,
> And the ripened state of long enjoyment.
> Therefore, at the start I praise compassion.

In this way, great Indian masters cite Shakyamuni Buddha's development of compassion to a limitless state as the ultimate reason why he is valued so highly.

Taking Refuge

According to the Great Vehicle, you go for refuge this way:

> Taking your own situation as an example, you contemplate the fact that although all sentient beings throughout space want happiness and do not want suffering, they have come under the influence of suffering, and seeking your own full enlightenment as an omniscient Buddha in order to help them, you go for refuge to the Three Jewels.

You can help this process along by meditating on and repeating
the following words:

> To the Buddha, the doctrine, and the supreme of
>   communities
> I go for refuge until enlightenment.
> Through the merit of the giving and so forth that I perform
> May I achieve Buddhahood in order to help transmigrating
>   beings.

Notice that the word *I* appears three times. When you repeat the
stanza, think about the nature of "I." There is no "I" that can be
pointed out as an entity separate from the mind-body complex;
not only that: if you carefully think about it, an "I" separate from
mind and body would involve many contradictions. In addition,
our own experience shows there is no such "I." Also, even if it may
seem to our mind that there is an "I" that is within mind and body
but is their controller like a head salesperson among salespersons,
that also does not exist. Therefore, in brief, the "I" cannot be found
when subjected to investigation, yet it undeniably exists, as when
we consider self and other; hence, the self, or "I," is merely set up
as a construct in dependence upon mind and body. If you reflect
on the nature of "I" while you recite the four lines given above, you
will establish helpful predispositions both in terms of motivational
compassion and in terms of the wisdom of selflessness.

Whether our actions of body, speech, and mind become virtuous, neutral, or nonvirtuous depends upon our motivation. Therefore, at the beginning of lectures on Buddhist doctrines, both the
lama and the students recite together this four-line formula for
seeking refuge in the Three Jewels and enhancing altruistic mo-

tivation. To avoid straying onto a wrong path we take refuge, and to avoid straying onto a self-centered path we find our motivation in an altruistic intention to become enlightened. Inasmuch as the lama can explain the doctrine within a positive attitude, the lama accumulates merit and its benefits; when students listen within a positive attitude, the doctrines they hear can move their minds, and through implementing the spiritual practices described they can achieve virtue. For these reasons both the lama and the students need to actively seek refuge.

A Triad of Practices

In his *Precious Garland of Advice,* Nagarjuna lays out the triad of practices that a follower of Buddha should take up:

> If you and the world wish to attain
> Unparalleled enlightenment,
> Its roots are the altruistic aspiration to enlightenment
> Firm like the monarch of mountains,
> Compassion reaching to all quarters,
> And wisdom not relying on duality.

Those who take refuge in Buddha should practice compassion, the wisdom realizing emptiness, and the altruistic intention to become enlightened. I practice these as much as I can and I have found over the course of my life that they are indeed very beneficial, making me happier and happier. Even if there were no future life, I would have no regrets; that these practices help in this life is sufficient. If there is a future life after this one, I am certain that the effort I have put into practicing altruism and the view of emptiness will have beneficial effects. Though I have not yet achieved control over how I will be reborn, if I continue these practices I will likely die with confidence that I can direct my own future rebirth.

Practicing compassion and the view of emptiness will be helpful to you as well; you will be happier. Many Buddhists meditate on special gods of wealth to try to get rich, medicine gods to improve their health, gods of long life to achieve longevity, and fierce gods for power, but altruism is the most effective tool for attaining all these things. Altruism puts your mind at ease. If your mind is at ease you will live longer, your body will be healthy, sickness and disease will diminish, and you will have many friends without having to resort to trickery or force.

Altruism built on love and compassion is the avenue to all these benefits. This is the beauty of Buddhism. But if you leave your afflictive emotions as they are, then even if you imagine a god of long life to your right, a god of wealth to your left, and a god of medicine in front of you, and you recite a mantra a billion times, still you will find it hard to achieve anything.

In Tibet there are hundreds of local gods, in whom the populace often places tremendous confidence. I sometimes tease Tibetans that in many temples there is an image of Shakyamuni Buddha in the center of the main hall to which people pay little attention, but in a separate area either to the side or upstairs is a special darkened room for the local protector gods who have huge mouths with fanged teeth, in front of whom people shrink in fear. Indeed, when you go to such rooms, it is almost as if you cannot breathe. Simply put, this reverence for local gods is a huge mistake. Confidence should be put in Buddha; he is the teacher of refuge, the ultimate protector.

Those who are properly training in the doctrine of Shakyamuni Buddha and have at least a minimal level of realization of emptiness and have attained some cessation of suffering are members of the spiritual community, and those who also have trained in altruism to the degree that they cherish others more highly than themselves are even more amazing. Even those who have not reached even these levels but are practicing with unshakable will are also sources of refuge.

Sources of refuge should be identified based on rational analysis with an unbiased attitude. As the Indian scholar Shamkarapati said:

I hold as teacher only
One whose word is endowed with reason.

For a teaching to be a suitable source of refuge, it must pass the scrutiny of reasoned reflection and must be highly beneficial. A famous Chilean scientist told me that a scientific researcher should not be attached to science, and I believe that in much the same way a Buddhist should not be attached to Buddhist doctrine as such, but instead should value teachings and teachers that can bear investigation into their validity. The scientific attitude and the Buddhist approach are the same in this case.

In sum, the realized doctrine is the actual refuge, the Buddha is the teacher of refuge, and the spiritual community helps you attain that refuge. Once you turn to these Three Jewels for refuge, you should refrain from doing harm to any living beings through thought or deed. Appreciate that all living beings have rights, not just humans.

IMAGES

It is important to value any image of the Buddha, whether it is fashioned from precious or ordinary material, constructed well or poorly. In the *Lotus Sutra* it is said that even nonbelievers who encounter an image of Buddha while emotionally worked up can have a tremendously beneficial experience. This is because Buddha's single-minded dedication from the depths of his heart to achieving the well-being of others, practicing the spiritual path of great compassion over eons and eons, generated an attitude so powerful that it even resides, in a sense, in images of him. Hence it is important not to consider these images as if they were just articles of furniture but rather to value them highly.

Contemplation

Consider these insights:

1. Mistaking people and things as having inherent existence gives rise to more mistaken thinking.

2. Mistaken thinking generates the afflictive emotions of lust, hatred, enmity, jealousy, belligerence, and laziness.

3. These destructive emotions lead to actions (karmas) that have been infected by these emotions.

4. These actions leave imprints in the mind that drive the painful round of repeated births.

5. Therefore, ignorance is the root of cyclic existence. Ignorance here means not just an absence of knowledge about how phenomena actually exist but an active misconception of the status of persons and things: seeing them as fully autonomous, or independent, entities.

6. This ignorance is uprooted by the realization that all phenomena are interrelated and interdependent entities.

7. If phenomena did indeed exist the way they appear to, that is, established on their own side, then, by definition, their dependence on other factors could not be possible, but your own experience shows you that interdependence is truly the way of things.

8. Through this route you can see that your own mental outlook mistakenly ascribes an exaggerated status to people and things; they do not exist in this way.

9. When you begin to see that this extreme assignment of virtue or evil to a person is what makes them an object of lust or hatred, the emotion that is built on that exaggeration backs off; we see the mistake we have made, and we pull back.

10. Good and bad, favorable and unfavorable do exist, but not in the concrete way that they seem to when viewed by a lustful or a hateful mind.

11. Once you understand that lust and hatred are mistakes and that their root, the ignorant conception that phenomena exist in their own right, is also mistaken, you will know that the wisdom that realizes dependent-arising and emptiness is founded in valid cognition.

12. When you cultivate this insight more and more, it will become stronger and stronger because it is valid, and you will see that enlightenment is possible.

13. You will see in your experience that reflecting on dependent-arising and emptiness engenders insight that is helpful in daily life, which can develop into an incontrovertible understanding of emptiness and even direct perception

of it. Even with a limited level of *valid experience* you can determine that there are *valid gurus* who can offer *valid commentaries* on Buddha's teachings, the *valid scriptures*. Based on these four validities, you can gain conviction in Buddhahood as profound and vast, as mentally and physically perfect.

14. By reflecting on the truth of dependent-arising and emptiness, you come to realize that it is possible to stop destructive thoughts through spiritual realizations in keeping with the Buddhist doctrine. Those who have some experience of these cessations and paths in their mental continua make up the spiritual community, and those who have brought this process of spiritual development to perfection are known as Buddhas. When these appear to your mind, you will see the reasonableness of turning to the Buddha, his doctrine, and the spiritual community for refuge.

15. Taking your own situation as an example, you contemplate the fact that although all sentient beings throughout space want happiness and do not want suffering, they have come under the influence of suffering; seeking your own full enlightenment as an omniscient Buddha in order to help them, you turn to the Three Jewels for refuge. The realized doctrine is the actual refuge; the Buddha is the teacher of refuge, and the spiritual community includes those who help you attain that refuge.

II

Karma

Just as the shadows of birds in the sky
Move along with them,
Beings are followed by
The right and wrong they have done.

—BUDDHA

Buddhism has two perspectives: worldly and transcendent. The
view of the emptiness of inherent existence is transcendent, and
the view of actions (karmas) and their effects is worldly. Looking
around this world and seeing that effects always arise in dependence upon their respective causes—and never independently—is
a major step toward achieving the transcendent view of the emptiness of inherent existence. With this in mind, Buddha taught,
"Whatever is produced from causes is not inherently produced."

All impermanent phenomena arise from causes, so they cannot be established under their own power; by relying on something
outside themselves they are naturally empty of an independent
existence. Although the correct worldly perspective of things as
dependent-arising is a coarser level of understanding, it serves
as a basis for realizing the transcendent perspective of subtle

dependent-arising, which contains the meaning of the emptiness of inherent existence.

Our topic in this chapter is karma, which concerns the correct worldly view of effects as arising dependent upon causes.

DEFINITENESS OF KARMA

All pleasures, small or great, arise from virtuous actions, whereas all pains, great or small, arise from nonvirtuous actions. In this sense, karma is unambiguous; in the long run good actions lead to happy states and bad actions lead to painful states. As Nagarjuna's *Precious Garland of Advice* says:

> From nonvirtues come all sufferings
> And likewise all bad transmigrations.
> From virtues, all happy transmigrations
> And the pleasures of all lives.

Karma is infallible in this way, but the effects of a given action can be subject to amplification. Among external phenomena a small seed can give rise to a great tree, and internal phenomena are subject to even greater magnification. Even small actions can lead to huge effects. For instance, uttering an ugly name to describe another person while motivated by anger can have effects over several lifetimes. Buddha said:

> Do not think that the cultivation
> Of even a tiny nonvirtue will not stay with you.
> Just as a large vessel is filled
> By drops of water falling,

So too is a fool filled with ill deeds
Accumulated a little at a time.

Do not think that the cultivation
Of even a tiny virtue will not stay you.
Just as a large pot is filled
By drops of water descending,
So too are the resolute filled by virtues
Accumulated a little at a time.

This means we should not be careless about what might appear to be deeds of little import, virtuous or nonvirtuous. Since no deed is clearly insignificant, take care even with the smallest deeds. Buddha said:

Do not disparage even the tiniest ill deed,
Thinking that it will do no harm.
Through the accumulation of drops of water
A great vessel gradually fills.

Because of the great power of actions, the fountainhead of all spiritual attainments is avoidance of the ten dark actions, which is also achievement of their opposites, the ten light actions. Buddha said:

These paths of the ten virtuous actions are the sources of birth as a human or as a god, the sources of attaining the goals of the virtuous endeavors of those still learning and of those with no more to learn, the sources of the enlightenment of the self-realized, the sources of all Bodhisattva deeds, and the sources of all Buddha qualities.

TYPES OF ACTIONS

Although in general *karma* means action, in this context *karma* refers to actions motivated by a specific intention. We engage in a limitless variety of such actions, carried out by way of body, speech, and mind based on an individual's intention. Nevertheless, the most important of these are contained in ten paths of actions, dark and light. As I outlined earlier, the three principal physical nonvirtues are killing, stealing, and sexual misconduct; the four principal verbal nonvirtues are lying, divisive talk, harsh speech, and senseless chatter; the three principal mental nonvirtues are covetousness, harmful intent, and wrong views. Let us consider these in more detail.

Among the three physical nonvirtues, killing is weightier than stealing, which in turn is weightier than sexual misconduct. Among the four verbal nonvirtues, lying is weightier than divisive talk, which is weightier than harsh speech, which is weightier than senseless chatter. Among the three mental nonvirtues, wrong views are weightier than harmful intent, which is weightier than covetousness. The same order of weightiness holds also for the ten opposite virtues, refraining from killing and so forth.

In addition, many factors influence the weight of virtuous and nonvirtuous actions:

- the intensity of your motivation
- habituation over a long time
- whether the action harms or helps people or groups that contribute to society
- how keen you have been with regard to those actions throughout your life

Also, actions become weightier depending on how they are done. For example, killing is weightier if you delight in it, encourage others to do it, perform the deed after much reflection and preparation, do it repeatedly, accomplish it through torture, make the victim perform unfit deeds, or do it when the victim is weak, in pain, poor, or piteously wailing.

TYPES OF EFFECTS OF KARMA

The effects of actions fall into several categories. For example, murder can lead to a rebirth in a miserable life as a hell-being, hungry ghost, or animal; this type of result is called a *fruitional effect*, because it affects an entirely new life. Then, after that unfortunate rebirth ends, if one is reborn as a human, for instance, that same earlier deed of killing can result in having a short life or in being subject to many illnesses; this is called an *experiential effect*. The same karma also can have a *functional effect*, such as liking to kill, as we see in little children who take delight in killing bugs. It can also produce *environmental effects*, such as rendering food, drink, and medicines weak and ineffective or even capable of promoting illness.

Correspondingly, a virtuous karma such as refraining from killing due to understanding its faults also can have a *fruitional effect* of being reborn in a happy transmigration as a human or god. As an *experiential effect* it can lead to a long life. As a *functional effect* it can give rise to disliking killing in a future life, and as an *environmental effect* it can result in living in an agreeable locale.

The karmas that fill out the details of a particular life situation can be either virtuous or nonvirtuous. For instance, even though a life as a human is the fruitional effect of a moral action, the effects of other, nonvirtuous karmas could bring to that human life poverty, illness, and an early death. Similarly, a nonvirtuous karma could impel rebirth as an animal, but virtuous karmas could bring about a long, healthy life in a loving household, which many dogs, cats, and birds enjoy.

Equality of the Sexes

Let me address an important issue. Certain Buddhist texts describe being male as a favorable karmic fruition, but they speak from the perspective of the time of their composition. However, today we live in an age when male and female are considered to be equal, and indeed male and female *are* equal and should have equal opportunity. Thus, being female is an equally favorable karmic fruition. Although Shakyamuni Buddha, from the perspective of his time, did speak of slight differences with regard to males and females, he also set forth the highest level of monastic vows for both monks and nuns. And in his Tantra teachings male and female are not only considered to be equal, but females are given special respect.

Some Buddhist texts describe the faults of a female body in order to reverse lust, but these texts were written for male practitioners, and the same understanding needs to be applied to the male body. Because Nagarjuna's *Precious Garland of Advice* was written for an Indian king, he speaks about the unclean substances in a woman's body, but after that he calls on the king to consider his own body in the same light.

I met a person who complained that Shantideva considered women to be inferior, and who cited as evidence that Shantideva lists many faults of women's bodies in his *A Guide to the Bodhisattva's Way of Life*; discouraged by this, the person who complained to me had turned away from studying that text. However, Shantideva was speaking to an assembly of monks, and thus as an antidote to lust for copulation he listed for that audience the physical problems with the object of such lust. When this is taken into account, we can see that his message is that women at risk of lust should apply exactly the same reflections with regard to the male body.

Ordination of Nuns

Since males and females are equal, it is important that full ordination for Buddhist nuns be restored in those countries where it has been lost. In China, Vietnam, and Taiwan such ordination survived, but it disappeared in Tibet. For the last twenty years we have been looking into how to revive this tradition among Tibetans. Some have said that the Dalai Lama should decide the matter, but the procedure for Buddhist monastic discipline requires that those upholding this training discuss the issue and democratically come to a conclusion. It is not a decision for any one person. In this light, it would be helpful if the Taiwanese who currently maintain the tradition of full ordination for women would take the issue to a Buddhist congress for discussion, analysis, and decision. This would benefit not only Tibet but also Thailand, Burma, and Sri Lanka, where the higher nuns' vows do not appear to exist in unbroken transmission from the past, and efforts to reintroduce or newly introduce those vows remain controversial. The issue is also pressing in Western countries, where a number of women have taken the lower vows and have interest in taking the higher ones. It is important for the Taiwanese to assume responsibility for bringing this issue to a pan-Buddhist monastic gathering.

What Tibetans in particular can contribute to the current situation of nuns is philosophical education, since our nuns have instituted the regular program of Tibetan philosophical studies for more than twenty years, and we are in the process of establishing the examination format for the Geshe degree, our Ph.D. equivalent.

THE ORDER OF THE EFFECTS OF KARMA

> The karmas that you have done will not disappear.
> Virtues and nonvirtues will give rise to their effects
> accordingly.
>
> —SHANTIDEVA

In terms of how and when karmas produce their effects, the weightiest ripen first. When those weights are equal, whatever karma is manifest at the time of death will ripen first. Because of this, it is important to remain calm during the process of dying; it is particularly important for friends to keep from moaning and crying at this time so as not to stir up attachment, making you want to remain in this life when it is your time to depart.

After the weightiest karmas and those of equal weight, the next to ripen are the major actions to which you are habituated. Among habits that are equally strong, those that formed earliest will ripen first.

As to when karmas will start to bear their fruit, nonvirtuous actions can begin ripening right in the present lifetime if they are performed in the following ways:

- with excessive attachment to your own body, resources, and life;
- with strong malice toward others;

- with enmity toward those who have helped you, refusing to reciprocate their kindness;
- with great animosity toward sources of refuge such as Buddha, the doctrine, the spiritual community, and gurus.

Similarly, virtuous actions can begin ripening right in the present lifetime if performed as follows:

- without mainly being concerned with your own body, resources, and life;
- with deep compassion and helpfulness;
- with a strong attitude of wishing to reciprocate help given to you;
- with deep faith and conviction.

Otherwise, the effects will be experienced in the next lifetime or in later lifetimes.

UNDERMINING THE EFFECTS OF KARMA

Once you have performed an action, whether virtuous or nonvirtuous, unless you counteract its potential you will definitely experience its effect, no matter how much time that takes. Even if it takes eons, the capacity of a karma to produce its effect will not be lost. About this, Buddha said:

Even in a hundred eons
A karma does not perish.
When the circumstances and the time arrive,
Beings surely will feel its effects.

Whether you have committed ill deeds
Or are committing them,
You will not escape suffering
Even if you tried to run away.

No matter where you stay, there is no place
That karma has not created,
Neither in the sky nor in the ocean,
Nor even in the midst of mountains.

Just as you will experience the effects of what you have done physically, mentally, or verbally, you will not experience the karmic effects, pleasant or unpleasant, of deeds you have not done. Nevertheless, the capacity of a virtuous deed to generate a good effect can be undermined by strong anger, which makes it important to control your rage so as to keep from undercutting the good effects of your actions. Fortunately, nonvirtues have one good quality: they are susceptible to purification. This is why it is crucial to engage in countermeasures that will diminish the effects of misdeeds. Let me explain how to do this.

If, for instance, you have committed an ill deed such as stealing, you can diminish its capacity to produce an effect, such as future poverty, through four practices, or ameliorating forces. The first is to develop contrition for the ill deed and to disclose it either to your peers or to a special figure such as your guru, or even to imagine telling it to Buddha and the Bodhisattvas. The key is that you can no longer hide what you have done.

The second practice is to undertake virtuous activities specifically for the sake of counteracting the impact of that misdeed, by engaging in charity or any other virtuous activity as long as it is aimed at undermining the effects of the ill deed. These virtues can be as wide-ranging as supporting schools or medical facilities, reading texts on wisdom, or expressing compassionate wishes for others. Cultivation of love and compassion are particularly effective at purifying ill deeds.

The third practice is to develop an intention not to engage in that ill deed in the future, to restrain yourself from doing so even at the risk of your life. The fourth is to establish a foundation in refuge and the altruistic intention to become enlightened. Just as a person who has fallen down on the ground must rise again on that ground, so ill deeds in relation to the Three Jewels are purified by going for refuge to them, and ill deeds in relation to sentient beings are purified by generating altruism toward sentient beings.

You cannot escape the effects of karmas if you have not engaged the four forces. With the help of these four forces, the effects of ill deeds can be avoided completely, or diminished such that small pains, such as a headache, occur instead of great suffering, or the duration of a negative effect can be shortened. The differences are relative to how effectively the four forces are cultivated.

Contemplation

Consider:

1. All pleasures, small or great, arise from virtuous actions, and all pains, great or small, arise from nonvirtuous actions.
2. Even small actions can have huge effects.
3. The three principal physical nonvirtues are killing, stealing, and sexual misconduct; the four principal verbal nonvirtues are lying, divisive talk, harsh speech, and senseless chatter; the three principal mental nonvirtues are covetousness, harmful intent, and wrong views.

4. Killing is weightier than stealing, which is weightier than sexual misconduct. Lying is weightier than divisive talk, which is weightier than harsh speech, which is weightier than senseless chatter. Wrong views are weightier than harmful intent, which is weightier than covetousness. The same order of weightiness holds also for the opposite virtues, refraining from killing and so forth.

5. Many factors influence the weight of virtuous and nonvirtuous actions: the intensity of motivation, habituation, whether the action harms or helps beneficial people or groups, and keenness for the action throughout your life.

6. Actions become weightier depending on how they are undertaken.

7. The effects of actions can take four aspects: fruitional, impelling an entire new life; experiental, or similar to the cause in experience; functional, or similar to the cause in a practical way; environmental, or similar to the cause in terms of external surroundings.

8. Although a happy transmigration as a human or god is a fruitional effect of a virtuous karma, and a bad transmigration as an animal, hungry ghost, or hell-being is a fruitional effect of a nonvirtuous karma, the karmas that fill out the details of that particular life situation can be either virtuous or nonvirtuous.

9. Among karmas, the weightiest ripen first, then karmas aroused at death, then the habituated karmas, followed by those that formed earliest.

10. Nonvirtuous karmas can begin ripening in the present lifetime if based on actions performed with excessive attach-

ment to your body, resources, and life, or with strong malice toward others, or with enmity toward those who have helped you, or with great animosity toward sources of refuge such as Buddha, the doctrine, and the spiritual community. Virtuous actions can begin ripening in the present lifetime if they were undertaken without being overly concerned with your own body, resources, and life, or if they were performed with deep compassion and helpfulness, or with a strong attitude of wishing to reciprocate for help given to you, or with deep faith and conviction. Otherwise, the effects will be experienced in the next lifetime or later lifetimes.

11. The force of virtuous deeds can be weakened by anger.

12. The capacity of a nonvirtuous karma to produce its effect will remain unless it is counteracted by the four forces: contrition, engaging in virtuous activities specifically for the sake of counteracting the impact of the nonvirtuous act, intending not to engage in it in the future, and building a foundation in refuge and the altruistic intention to become enlightened.

THE IMPACT

In sum, by reflecting repeatedly on:

- impermanence
- the certainty and imminence of death
- the quality of your future lives
- and the power of karma

overemphasis on the present will turn into a more long-term concern. When these attitudes become your stable outlook, you have completed development of the first level of practice, and you are ready to rise to the next level.

Next let us take a deeper look at what it means to seek freedom from all types of cyclic existence.

MIDDLE LEVEL OF PRACTICE

12

Seeing the Problem and the Cure

I as teacher show you the path
To stop the pains of cyclic existence.
You have to implement it.

—BUDDHA

By reflecting on the effects of your actions and avoiding nonvirtues, you can achieve a good future life in cyclic existence, but that aim, despite being on the first rung of practice, does not constitute the full measure of Buddhist motivation. For once you understand the causes and effects of karma, you need to learn to turn away from all levels of cyclic existence. But although the purpose of avoiding the ten nonvirtues, introduced on the initial level of practice, is to achieve a favorable life within cyclic existence, this does not conflict with the middle-level teaching that even high status in cyclic existence has a nature of suffering and is to be forsaken. You need a favorable form of life to attain liberation, so if you do not free yourself from cyclic existence in this life, you will need a well-endowed life in the future to fulfill your own and others' aims.

On the middle level of capacity, you develop the motivation to leave all levels of cyclic existence, which serves as the doorway to the highest level of motivation, that of aspiring to enlightenment for the sake of helping others. This is because training in motivation for complete freedom from cyclic existence opens the way to developing a profound sense of altruism. I will explain how this works in this chapter and the next.

IDENTIFYING LIBERATION

No matter how wonderful a state you might achieve within cyclic existence, you are still under the control of destructive emotions and karma, which means that eventually you must fall from that fantastic state. To consider it to be the ultimate object of attainment is to be deceived by an illusion.

What then is liberation? Some philosophies of India do not accept the possibility of freedom from the round of birth, aging, sickness, and death, whereas others do. Among the latter, some assert that liberation is like a heaven, but Buddhists hold that liberation is a quality of mind, a mental state free from the bondage of painful emotions and karmas (actions) driven by them. Please bear with me while I explain this in some detail.

Living beings are bound up in a process in which mind and body fall under the influence of afflictive emotions and corresponding counterproductive karmas that bind them in lives as gods, demigods, humans, animals, hungry ghosts, and hell-beings, all of which are temporary states driven by karma. The way out of this situation is to put an end to afflictive emotions; this way karmas that have accumulated in your mind stream from countless lives in cyclic existence cannot be activated, and hence cannot manifest as a new lifetime of suffering. Then the karmas remaining in your mental continuum lose their potential to do harm. Liberation, therefore, is a state of separation from living under the control of afflictive emotions and karma. For more detail, let us look at Buddha's central teaching of the four noble truths.

The Core Perspective

Just as you recognize that you are ill
And see that you can eliminate the cause of illness
By attaining health through relying on a remedy,
So recognize suffering,
Eliminate its cause,
Attain its cessation,
And rely on the path.

—MAITREYA, *SUBLIME*
CONTINUUM OF THE
GREAT VEHICLE

Buddha became enlightened in Varanasi, India, and after several weeks gave his initial teaching, which was on the four noble truths. This is his rubric for identifying mistaken attitudes and for producing their antidotes. The foundation of the four truths is the view of dependent-arising, which itself is founded on selflessness.

Proper understanding of the four truths is crucial. In brief:

- All phenomena based on afflictive emotions and karma lead to sufferings; this is the first noble truth.
- Afflictive emotions and the actions (karmas) they motivate are the true origins of suffering; this is the second noble truth.
- Putting an end to afflictive emotions, the source of pain, is liberation; cessation is the third noble truth.
- The paths, or means, to overcoming and pacifying afflictive emotions are true paths; this is the fourth noble truth.

In terms of the order in which these four come into being, the sources of suffering (the second truth) come first, since they give rise to suffering (the first truth). Similarly, the spiritual paths (the fourth truth) allow us to attain the cessation of suffering, as well as to extinguish its sources (the third truth), since practice of the paths finally leads to true freedom. However, when Buddha taught the four truths, he reversed the order, speaking first about suffering (the effect), and then its sources (or causes). Likewise, he spoke first about putting an end to suffering and then also the paths that are the means of attaining this cessation.

He did this in order to drive home the essentials of practice. First, you need to reflect on the scope of *suffering*, including in particular the pain of pervasive conditioning, discussed earlier (p. 41). Once you realize the full scope of suffering, you investigate the *sources* of such pain, identifying the three poisonous emotions of lust, hatred, and ignorance. Ignorance, which here is specifically a belief in inherent existence, is the root of all destructive emotions. Whether these poisons can be transcended depends on whether antidotes exist for them. When you see that not only is there an antidote but it can be cultivated into a limitless state, you develop a strong wish to bring about the *cessation* of suffering and its origins. With this background, you then train in the *path* of morality, concentrated meditation, and wisdom, and, in particular, in the union of a highly focused mind and direct insight into selflessness. The nature of this process is the reason for Buddha's laying out the four truths in this order.

Identification of the scope of suffering is crucial for the full development of compassion. If you do not develop a strong intention to escape the clutches of the suffering of pervasive conditioning after seeing its pernicious works, the development of thoroughgoing compassion will lie beyond your reach. All of us possess the seeds of compassion, for when we see those close to us in pain we are immediately concerned, but when we see others whose pleasurable situation is just part of the suffering of changeability, far from wanting them to gain freedom from it, we ourselves admire it and even become jealous of it. Because we have not fully identified the scope of suffering, our compassion is limited. Thus, to develop compassion and, in particular, great compassion, it is crucial to first identify the suffering of pervasive conditioning in our own life.

Counterproductive emotions are unpeaceful, uncomfortable, stressful, and disturbing. If you leave these forces as they are, they will continue to produce pain, which is why they need to be extinguished by way of a powerful antidote. Once they are no more, you have reached true cessation, so the powerful antidote is the true path.

When you live under the outside influence of afflictive emotions, you have lost your independence and are trapped in cyclic existence; conquest of these harmful enemies yields independence, liberation. To orient yourself toward seeking liberation you need to know the defects of cyclic existence. Then you will wholeheartedly seek to undermine afflictive emotions, which moves you toward attaining liberation.

As the First Panchen Lama, Losang Chökyi Gyaltsen, said in the sixteenth century:

> With respect to how to reflect on the defects of cyclic existence, among the many ways of doing so even animals fear outright pain and want freedom from it, and even non-Buddhists turn away from pleasures that can change into pain. Therefore, this

mind-body complex that has a nature of being under the control of afflictive emotions and karma is to be seen as the basic condition for inducing all types of suffering in the future and hence is to be transcended.

The essential point of developing an intention to leave cyclic existence is to separate from the destructive emotions that keep mind and body bound up in this uncontrolled process. When this intention becomes your driving motivation, you rise to the middle level of spiritual capacity.

There are many Indian religious systems that involve strong devotion to the guru, and there are many adherents who totally dedicate their lives to spiritual practice. They are impressive. Mindful of the impermanence of this life, they put great effort into religious devotion. But only Buddhism sees the very apprehension of self to be faulty, and instead puts forth a view of selflessness. Only when you view as faulty the conception of self and the destructive emotions induced by this wrong idea are you inside the door of actual Buddhist practice; this is why the four noble truths are so central.

THE TRUTH OF SUFFERING

Since we justifiably want happiness and do not want suffering, we naturally focus on pleasure and pain, which is why Buddha first identified what suffering actually is. At that time in India non-Buddhist systems certainly had focused on obvious physical and mental pain, and it is likely that they also had identified the way that overuse of a seeming source of pleasure turns into pain, like eating too much tasty food. However, it is extremely difficult to identify the deeper suffering of pervasive conditioning, which is based on the fact that our mind and body do not operate completely under our own control but fall under the influence of karmas (previous actions and the tendencies created by them), which themselves are driven by destructive emotions such as lust and hatred.

Look at it this way. We lust after pleasurable forms, sounds, odors, tastes, and touches, and anger arises when this lust is thwarted, whether due to an interfering person or outside circumstances. Non-Buddhist texts teach that such lust is faulty as well as ways to counter these destructive attitudes, but they do not describe the drawbacks of mistaking the self and other phenomena for existing autonomously in their own right, so they do not identify the more subtle levels of lust and hatred rooted in this subtler misconception. Buddha, however, taught about the suffering of pervasive conditioning, which is that ordinary mind and body, at root, are generated from misapprehension of inherent existence and are caught in a round of suffering even when outright physical and mental pain are not manifest.

Prior to Buddha there were those who identified suffering, but without recognizing the subtler causes of deprivation we cannot truly appreciate the scope of suffering in cyclic existence. As the Tibetan scholar-yogi Tsongkhapa says in his *Great Treatise on the Stages of the Path:*

Buddhas' trainees, obstructed by the darkness of ignorance, were deceived through mistaking the wonderful things of cyclic existence—which in fact involve suffering—for happiness, and thus they needed to generate disenchantment with these things. Therefore, Buddha spoke of many forms of suffering, saying "These in reality are not happiness but suffering." This is why he initially set forth the truth of suffering.

Due to mistaking the true nature of persons (including other living beings such as animals) and also to mistaking what is impure for pure, what is a state of pain for pleasure, and what is impermanent for permanent, we bring trouble upon ourselves. This is why it is necessary to identify the full scope of suffering. Buddha called this insight "the noble truth of suffering" because this is how the actual state of our condition appears to those who see the actual situation just as it is. For instance, ordinary beings usually view pleasurable feelings as beneficial without further thought, whereas in the sight of those who know the actual situation even ordinary pleasures are seen as part of the cycle of suffering brought about by change.

The Pain of Birth

In general, cyclic existence has many shortcomings. First, consider the suffering of birth. There are various types of strong discomfort we experience while still in the womb, before we even emerge, which involve a great deal of pain for both mother and child. After birth you are held upside down and slapped on the behind to help clear the lungs, which means that life outside the womb starts with the torment of being hung by the heels and hit.

In the area of Amdo Province in northeastern Tibet where I was born, there is a custom among country folk of giving a baby a potion made from licorice root. My older sister told me that I drank a huge amount of it, perhaps indicating that in my mother's womb I was experiencing the pain of hunger. Beyond that, there is pernicious suffering due to the simple fact that the body with which we are born is already associated with dysfunctional tendencies. Because our body itself is born from afflictive emotions and karma, it is naturally at odds with achieving virtue.

In Tibetan medicine the basic forces of our bodies consist of three humors—wind, bile, and phlegm—that need to be kept in balance for good health but are easily imbalanced and hence are literally called "the three problems." All the internal causes of disease and aging already exist within the body from the start.

Our birth, which derives from afflictive emotions and karma, means that we are already prone to those same afflictive emotions, generating lust for what find attractive, hatred for what we find unattractive, and confusion about everything else. From the day we are born we undergo many calamities ending in death, and then from the day of the next birth it is the same. If there is a way of eliminating all these problems, surely it should be considered.

The Pain of Aging

It is well that aging happens little by little.
If it happened all at once, it would be intolerable.

—GAMAPA, TIBETAN YOGI

With aging, your fine body deteriorates. Strength weakens. The senses decline. Enjoyments fade. And finally, life is exhausted. Buddha said:

Aging steals our vigor, skill, and strength
Till we seem we are stuck in mud.

The Pain of Illness

Just as humans oppress wild animals,
Hundreds of illnesses and pains of rampant disease afflict us.
—BUDDHA

With illness, your skin dries out, and your flesh wastes away. Be-cause the physical elements your body comprises are out of bal-ance, you face physical pain that in turn promotes mental pain. You cannot indulge your wants. You have to undergo unpleasant treatments. Your vitality weakens. Buddha said:

In deep winter, great winds and blizzards
Take the vigor from grasses, shrubs, trees, and herbs.
In the same way, disease takes the vigor out of living beings,
Breaking down their faculties, physical appearance, and
strength.

Finally, you are pained by seeing that your illness will not be cured.

The Pain of Death

With death, you suffer from seeing that you will be separated from fine objects, fine relatives, and fine friends, and as you die, you un-dergo many discomforts. As Buddha said:

When you die and pass on to another life,
You are forever separated from persons beautiful and beloved.
Like a leaf fallen from a tree or the current of a river,
You will never return and meet them again.

Becoming Disenchanted with Cyclic Existence

On top of the sufferings of birth, aging, sickness, and death, we encounter the pains of facing the unpleasant, separating from the pleasant, and not finding what we want. During most of life we are confronted by unfavorable circumstances, one after another, day by day, in response to which we generate counterproductive emotions, specifically lust, hatred, and confusion, which produce similar suffering in the future. We are all faced with:

- the uncertainty of our friends and enemies, as they switch from one category to another in this life and over the course of countless lifetimes. As Tsongkhapa says:

    By meditating on this, you should stop generating both the attachment and the hostility that come from discriminating between friends and enemies.

- lack of contentment, because even though we seek pleasure, no matter how many comforts we gain we are insatiable, thereby bringing on ourselves the terrible pain of forever always seeking greater comfort. As Tsongkhapa says:

    You indulge in pleasures in pursuit of satisfaction, yet with transitory pleasures you are never satisfied no matter how much you enjoy them. Time after time your craving grows, and on that account you wander for ages in cyclic existence.

- the problem of casting aside our body from life to life. As Nagarjuna says:

    Each of us has left behind a pile of bones
    That would dwarf the greatest mountain.

- the problem of being born again and again. Nagarjuna says:

After even having become monarch of the universe,
You will once again become others' slave in cyclic
existence.

- the problem of descending from a high level to a low level
over and over even within a single lifetime. As Buddha says:
The end of accumulation is depletion.
The end of height is falling.
The end of meeting is separation.
The end of life is death.

- the problem of not having constant companions over the
course of lifetimes, going from life to life by yourself. Shantideva says:
You are born alone.
You also die alone.

In brief, the basic problem lies with the type of mind and body
that we have. Our mind-body complex serves as a basis for present
sufferings in the form of aging, sickness, and death, and promotes
future suffering through our usual responses to painful situations.

By reflecting on birth and on the nature of mind and body, you
will be moved from the depths of your heart to seek relief, thinking, "If I could only be free from a life driven by afflictive emotions
and karma!" Without such reflection on pain, your knowledge of
your own condition will be limited, which itself will put a limit on
your compassion. As Tsongkhapa says:

If you do not cultivate a genuine sense of disenchantment with
cyclic existence—whose nature is a mind-body complex under
the sway of afflictive emotions and karma—you will have no

chance to develop a genuine attitude intent on liberation, and there will be no way to develop great compassion for beings wandering in cyclic existence. Therefore, it is crucial to reflect on your situation.

We can see from our own experience that all forms of suffering are contained in our present human life. As Vasubandhu says:

It is apparent that humans also have
All the sufferings of miserable life forms.
Tormented by pain, humans are like hell-beings.
Deprived, we are like hungry ghosts.
Humans also have the suffering of animals
In that the powerful use force
To hurt and oppress the weak.
These sufferings are just like a river.
Some suffer from poverty;
Others, from discontent;
The pangs of yearning are unbearable;
All quarrel and are subject to murder.

A human life is certainly desirable for the sake of continuing practice, but if even this precious human life is beset with such terrible problems, imagine the suffering of other life forms!

THE TRUTH OF THE ORIGINS OF SUFFERING

If you want to get rid of painful effects, you have to get rid of their causes, which is why Buddha next taught the truth about the origins of pain. If those causes and conditions are not overcome, the suffering they create cannot be overcome.

What are the causes of suffering? If suffering were created by a permanent cause, there would be no way to overcome it, since a permanent cause would not be subject to change. Fortunately, suffering is a dependent-arising, produced in dependence upon impermanent causes and conditions. Because the causes themselves are in a process of change, the suffering produced by them is subject to alteration. This is why Buddha taught that if the causes are mutable, their effects are also mutable.

In ordinary life, when we are faced with pain from sickness, aging, death, and various kinds of loss, this pain cannot be eliminated as soon as it occurs because it arises dependent upon its respective causes and conditions. However, by seeking out and striving to counteract those causes we can bring about elimination of the particular pain, resulting in greater physical comfort, freedom from a particular illness, longer life, more resources, and good companions. To accomplish this, we require education. In general in the world, people seek an education not for the sake of future lives but to reduce pain and increase pleasure in this life itself. When people advance in their training, they become more effective at behaving in ways that actually remove the ills of this life and achieve its pleasures.

We learn how to reduce suffering and enhance happiness by adjusting the way we think, since aspiring to change precedes implementing those techniques that lead to change—the wish to act must come before action. Indeed, certain smaller actions, such as immediately rubbing an itch or shutting your eyes when they are in danger, happen instinctively, but most actions involving significant benefit require the thought "I should do this." These actions require intention, or will; on that platform we perform actions of body and speech.

So pleasure and pain in this life arise in dependence upon actions, which themselves depend upon thought. Actions derive from motivation. For instance, ordinarily when you oppose someone, you first generate a sense of dislike or hatred for the person, thinking, "He is making trouble for me. I have to oppose him." Having generated these ideas, you consider how to confront this person, what strategy to use. When specific approaches dawn in your mind, you develop the intention, the will, to carry them out, and then you implement them. Thus there are two stages involved: first comes the motivating hatred, followed by action. The same is true in situations of desire. First you generate a strong liking for the object or person, and then motivated by this feeling you consider how to get what you want and act accordingly.

This is our general procedure—this is how we act. In the second noble truth, Buddha points out that starting with a defective attitude about self leads to other destructive emotions—mainly lust and hatred. These, in turn, motivate counterproductive actions, producing suffering. It is all a matter of cause and effect.

Afflictive Emotions

What produces the suffering experienced in the cycle of birth, aging, sickness, and death? Contaminated actions. What produces contaminated actions? The destructive emotions of lust and hatred. What is their root? Ignorance, specifically a mistaken idea of inherent existence. Therefore, between the two origins of suffering, contaminated actions and afflictive emotions, afflictive emotions are primary, and among those counterproductive emotions, ignorance is chief.

Afflictive emotions are defined as any attitude that makes your mental continuum unpeaceful. When an attitude such as strong compassion is generated, for instance, it does indeed ruffle the mind a little, but it does so intentionally through a series of reflections that elevate your mind. Conversely, even though generating afflictive emotions does sometimes involve some slight resort to reason, it is the nature of afflictive emotions to disturb the mind beyond your own control, beyond the realm of intention or reflection. They stir you up and make you uncomfortable.

Among these destructive emotions is lust, which comes from observing a pleasant and attractive external phenomenon (an enjoyable object, or fame, a residence, or a friend) or internal phenomenon (such as the shape, color, touch, or scent of your own body) and becoming attached to it. Actually, whether such external or internal objects are pleasant can be determined only in the context of a consciousness endowed with discrimination and feeling. It is difficult to say that an object is pleasant and attractive outside of such a context. That is why we say, "This is good looking *to me*" or "This is appealing *to me*."

Pleasant and unpleasant are subjective, determined by a person or, more specifically, by a particular consciousness. In actual fact, however, it remains an open question whether the object is pleasant or unpleasant, whether it is helpful or not. Thoughts exaggerate the qualities of an object deemed desirable to the point where it is completely enticing, drawing your mind into it like oil soaking into cloth. It is as if your mind dissolved into the desired object, thoroughly mixing with it, making it difficult to separate from it.

The psychologist I mentioned earlier said that when we generate lust and hatred, 80 to 90 percent of that perception is over-blown, inflated by thought. This is exactly the same notion found in Buddhist texts about exaggerated attitudes that we call "super-impositions by unfounded modes of thought," or more simply, fanciful creations of foolishness.

Nevertheless, good and bad do exist; the helpful is good, and the harmful is bad. It is difficult to determine good and bad except in relation to feelings of pleasure and pain, but we need to discriminate further. We need to become disenchanted with cyclic existence and to aspire to attain liberation. Desire falls into two basic types: afflictive and nonafflictive. When, for instance, it is said that we should have few desires and be content, these desires are non-afflictive; the other type, built on exaggeration, is afflictive.

In a similar way, hatred is a riled-up state of mind that is based on exaggeration (of another person, of your own pain, or even of a cause of pain such as a thorn) that makes it seem more unpleasant than it really is; hatred rages against that object and drives us to do harm to it. Nevertheless, a strong dislike of afflictive emotions that gets you worked up about them is beneficial since, like strong compassion, it arises from reflecting on well-founded observations, not from an afflictive emotion that is out of control. It is important to make these distinctions between afflictive and nonafflictive attitudes.

IGNORANCE LEADS TO OTHER AFFLICTIVE EMOTIONS

In sum, both lust and hatred develop based on an ignorant exaggeration of the nature of things far beyond what is actually there. This ignorance spawns all other afflictive emotions. When it mistakenly considers that you yourself exist as a fully independent entity, this engenders an artificial distinction between self and other. This bifurcation encourages becoming attached to what is on your own side and resistance to what is on the side of others, which opens the door to pride, to inflating your own actual or imagined qualities such as wealth, education, physical appearance, ethnic origin, and fame.

When an afflictive emotion is engendered, independence is lost. At least for the time being, your own mind is disturbed, which weakens your capacity for judgment. When strong desire or hatred are generated, you forget to analyze whether an action is suitable or not, and can even speak crazily and make wild gestures. Then, when that emotion fades, you end up embarrassed and sorry for what you have done. This shows us that during the strong emotion, your capacity to distinguish between good and bad, suitable and unsuitable, was lost, and you came under the full control of that lust or hatred.

At that time, because you were worked up, you created additional discomfort among those around you. When someone gets angry, even bystanders feel discomfort, and intimates are saddened and disturbed. If hateful actions are taken, the disturbance spreads. In this way, afflictive emotions ruin your life and the lives of others in your family, community, or society. So we see that all of the many upsets that are so prevalent in the world stem from the three poisons of lust, hatred, and ignorance. As Tsongkhapa says:

> When an afflictive emotion arises, at first it thoroughly afflicts your mind, causing you to err with regard to what you are observing, reinforcing your latent proclivities, and caus-

ing the same sort of destructive emotion to recur. It may harm you, others, or both; it leads to misdeeds in this life, in future lives, or both. It creates experiences of pain and anguish, as well as the sufferings of rebirth in cyclic existence and so forth. It takes you far from nirvana, your virtue is destroyed, and your resources are depleted. In society you feel apprehensive, joyless, and devoid of confidence.

Whether you believe in religion or not, it is important to identify these destructive tendencies for what they are. Poison needs to be recognized as poison. If you do not see them clearly, you might view these outbursts as just a natural part of living, rather than signs that you are trapped in counterproductive behavior. They are simply harmful to both yourself and others.

The fact is that suffering from mental and physical pain, change, or pervasive conditioning arises when we fall under the influence of misconceptions about the nature of people and other phenomena. This is the message of the second noble truth, the truth about the origins of pain.

THE TRUTH OF CESSATION

The third noble truth involves cessation. Tsongkhapa says:

> Since when you see that the conception of self can be eliminated, you will undertake to actualize its cessation, Buddha next set forth the truth of cessation.

What is cessation? When we generate an antidote to a particular cause, it stops, whereupon the effects of that cause are not produced. The term *cessation* or *stoppage* itself indicates that what is stopped does not cease of its own accord but through exertion. If the cause is left as is, it will continue unabated, producing its effects. However, by making an effort to generate its antidotes, you undermine the cause, and you are freed from its effects. As the Tibetan meditator Potowa said:

> For as long as we have wandered through cyclic existence in the past it has not stopped by itself. Given this, it will not stop by itself now either. Hence, we must put a stop to it, and the time to do so is today.

Through your own exertions you must put a stop to the destructive emotions that cause suffering, and thereby put an end to actions contaminated by those destructive emotions. If left as they are, they will repeatedly produce suffering.

How can counterproductive emotions be stopped? Through exerting an opposing force. Most, if not all, external phenomena have opposing forces, such as heat and cold. The presence of opposing forces creates the possibility of change; therefore, when you need to counteract something, you first identify its opposing force; when you increase its power, the strength of its opposite diminishes. For example, when we turn on a fan or air conditioner, the feeling of heat diminishes; we have intentionally increased cold, which is the opposite of heat.

The same is true for internal attitudes. For instance, desire draws an object close, whereas anger turns us away from it. In ordinary life, pleasure and pain are mainly associated with the body; desire draws together those factors that sustain and give pleasure to the body, whereas anger wards off factors that harm the body.

Desire draws things together, whereas anger separates and pushes apart.

What is the problem with lust and hatred? Although the drawing together of helpful factors is needed, lustful desire is biased, exaggerating the favorable qualities of an object at the expense of seeing the actual situation, so actions based on this distorted attitude inevitably produce trouble. Worse still, hatred is always in the wings. Sympathetic love, however, is not based on a misconception. Sympathetic love stems from reflecting on meaning and purpose and therefore arises from clear discernment of the situation. It is based on true consideration of the other person.

Although unfavorable conditions need to be removed, when they are removed with hatred, this means of relief creates its own problems, because hatred, colored by its bias, does not see the true situation. But just as favorable conditions can be successfully achieved by sympathetic love without generating afflictive emotions, so can unfavorable conditions can be removed by wisdom, that is, by analyzing the facts and discerning the actual situation.

So just as we treat an unfavorable external phenomenon by seeking out its opposite and increasing its power, we take an unwanted mental phenomenon's opposite and increase it. Opposition here means that the two attitudes are contradictory, as is the case with sympathetic love and hatred, which unite and separate respectively.

Opposition opens the way for transformation. When the causes of suffering are afflictive emotions, turning to attitudes that oppose them promotes healthy change. As you turn to them more and more, these attitudes strengthen because they are reasonable and true, whereas afflictive emotions—despite being strong because we are so used to them—diminish in the face of analysis.

Counterproductive emotions are based on ignorant misapprehension of the nature of oneself, others, and things, and since such ignorance is mistaken, all attitudes that it spawns are also mistaken. No matter how strong afflictive emotions become, they are misguided. For instance, when a state of pain is mistaken for pleasure or when something that is impermanent is seen to be permanent, these perspectives are mistaken, which means their opposites are founded in reason. These opposing attitudes are mutually exclusive, since one side is not founded in valid cognition whereas the other is, and the one becomes weaker over time while the other becomes stronger and stronger when you train in it.

Whether the causes of suffering cease or not depends on whether or not the mind is tamed. When you understand this, you will become determined to tame your mind and actualize cessation, as Buddha indicated.

In sum, the causes of the deepest level of suffering are afflictive emotions, which are rooted in the ignorant idea of inherent existence. This ignorance can be effectively counteracted by its antidote. In general, once a powerful countermeasure is applied to something impermanent, that phenomenon can be eliminated. Simply knowing that our view of inherent existence is mistaken can counter this misperception and eventually eliminate it.

Enlightenment carries with it a sense of purification or cleansing, which means liberation from pain by generating an antidote. That state of having been purified is called "cessation," which is the third noble truth. When you understand that this removal of unwanted problems is possible, you will develop a desire to actualize this state.

THE TRUTH OF PATHS

How can we attain separation from the causes of suffering? This cannot be done by prayer or wishes alone. Even limited results require exertion. Without effort, achievement is impossible. For example, when we want to eat a meal, we cannot get it by lying down and just wishing for it; we have to buy groceries and cook them. In order to be free of suffering ,we must exert ourselves to a far greater degree. When you see this, your resolve strengthens to implement the techniques, the paths, leading to freedom.

Chief among these techniques is the direct realization of self-lessness, for this is the antidote to the mistaken view that is the source of suffering. It requires special training in wisdom, and in order to so powerfully penetrate reality, it is necessary to train in concentrated meditation, which, in turn, rests on training in morality. The paths to freedom are structured as three trainings: morality, concentrated meditation, and wisdom.

Morality restrains harmful actions based on self-protection, which, when it becomes effective, brings with it a capacity to keep track of internal motivation. Then, the training in concentrated meditation increases this mental capacity by focusing its force, which was previously scattered, onto a single object. Using concentrated meditation, the mind can focus on the true nature of things, thereby supporting the training in wisdom. With wisdom, you can be more effective at helping others. Because these techniques—the three trainings of morality, concentrated meditation, and wisdom—are the way out of the cycle of pain, they are called the truth of paths.

Contemplation

Consider:

1. Mind and body fall under the influence of destructive emotions, and the actions (karmas) driven by these counterproductive attitudes bind beings in temporary states as gods, demigods, humans, animals, hungry ghosts, and hell-beings.

2. The way out of this situation is to address afflictive emotions directly, which keeps previously accumulated karmas from being activated so they cannot manifest as a new lifetime of suffering. The karmas remaining in your mental continuum are thereby deactivated.

3. Liberation is a state of separation from the burden of living with a mind and body under the control of destructive emotions and karma.

4. There are four noble truths:

   - External and internal phenomena that are fashioned from destructive emotions and karma are true sufferings.

   - Afflictive emotions and karmas are the true origins of suffering.

   - Pacification of afflictive emotions is liberation, or true cessation.

   - The means for overcoming and pacifying afflictive emotions are known as true paths.

5. The first two of the four truths, suffering and its sources, indicate what we need to discard; the last two, cessations and paths, point out what we need to adopt.

6. Since all of us want happiness and do not want suffering, we must *recognize* the full extent of suffering, for then we will seek liberation from it. Once we decide we do not want these

painful effects, we must *abandon* the destructive emotions that cause them, the sources of suffering. In order to achieve a cure we need to *actualize* the cessation of the sources of pain. To do this, we must *cultivate* the path.

7. If you do not have a strong intention to escape the clutches of pervasive conditioning by looking at its pernicious works, the development of thoroughgoing compassion will lie beyond your reach.

8. Counterproductive emotions are unpeaceful, uncomfortable, stressful, and disturbing.

9. Lust leads to anger when it is thwarted.

10. We bring trouble upon ourselves by mistaking the true nature of people, but also mistaking what is impure for pure, what is a state of pain for pleasure, and what is impermanent for permanent.

11. Our birth from afflictive emotions and karma means that we are prone to those same emotions, generating lust for the attractive, hatred for the unattractive, and confusion for what is neither.

12. If aging happened all at once, it would be intolerable.

13. Sickness puts the elements of the body out of balance, bringing physical pain that in turn promotes mental pain, which weakens vitality and makes fulfillment impossible.

14. We suffer from seeing that death will separate us from nice objects, nice relatives, and nice friends, and while dying we may undergo many discomforts.

15. Our mind-body complex serves as a basis for present suffering (projected by earlier afflictive emotions and karmas) that plays itself out in aging, sickness, and death, and our usual responses to painful situations promote future suffering.

16. By being associated with dysfunctional tendencies, our mind-body complex induces outright suffering; the very existence of this sort of mind and body is itself an expression of the suffering of pervasive conditioning.

17. Since pain and pleasure arise from causes and conditions, these feelings are subject to techniques that bring relief.

18. Between the two origins of suffering, contaminated actions and afflictive emotions, afflictive emotions (lust, hatred, and ignorance) are the primary cause, and among those counter-productive emotions ignorance is chief because lust and hatred arise from exaggeration of the status of an object beyond what actually exists.

19. When you see that this ignorance can be eliminated because it lacks the support of valid cognition, you become determined to tame your mind to achieve what is known as cessation.

20. The presence of opposing forces indicates the potential for change; when you need to counteract something, first you identify its opposing force, and when you increase its power, the strength of its opposite diminishes. Since suffering is caused by afflictive emotions, relying on attitudes that oppose them promotes healthy change.

21. Chief among the paths leading to freedom is direct realization of selflessness (the emptiness of inherent existence) because this has the power to serve as an actual antidote to the source of suffering. This special training in wisdom requires concentrated meditation, which in turn depends on training in morality. Thus the amelioration of suffering relies on three trainings—morality, concentrated meditation, and wisdom.

13

The Implications of Impermanence

Would a sick person be helped
Merely by reading a medical text?

—SHANTIDEVA

We already have the fortunate inner circumstances that allow
for practice, and we need to notice this because knowledge of its
value will influence us not to waste it. However, procrastination
can easily interfere with our intention to make good use of the situation. The prescription for ending delay is meditation on impermanence, so in this chapter I will explore this important practice
more deeply.

In teaching the four noble truths, Buddha began by speaking
about suffering, calling attention to impermanence. Similarly,
when he set forth his philosophical view in four aphorisms, he first
spoke of impermanence:

All compounded things are impermanent.
All things contaminated with afflictive emotions are
miserable.
All phenomena are selfless.
Nirvana is peace.

The reason for emphasizing reflection on impermanence is that so many of the problems and troubles we run into are created by our mistaking for permanent that which is actually impermanent. To understand this important topic, we first need to make a distinction between coarse and subtle impermanence. All of us notice the changes that take place in the seasons, our bodies, and so on; these are examples of coarse impermanence. For instance, when a cup breaks, the continuum of moments of its existence ends, and when a person dies, the stream of moments of that particular life ceases.

We notice change over a span of weeks, or months, or years, such coarse alterations being undeniable, but these large-scale changes are the result of much smaller and less obvious moment-by-moment changes. From the existence of gross changes we can infer that things change moment by moment; this is subtle impermanence.

In the four noble truths and the four aphorisms, Buddha is referring to subtle impermanence, the moment-by-moment disintegration of anything that has a cause. When you contemplate subtle impermanence deeply, you understand that things caused by something else have a nature of mutability from their very onset. Bear with me while I explain this in terms of the above four aphorisms; this knowledge has tremendous impact.

THE FIRST APHORISM

Buddhist texts on reasoning repeatedly emphasize that whatever is made by causes and conditions is necessarily impermanent. When we examine this statement, it may seem that there is a disjunction between the two parts, "made by causes and conditions" and "impermanent." Being made by causes and conditions indicates that something is newly established, whereas impermanence indicates that something ceases, stops, disintegrates. Establishment and ceasing appear to have different imports, but as we reflect further we see that the fact that something is made itself means that it has a nature of disintegrating at every moment.

From its onset, a phenomenon has the character of impermanence since it ceases that very moment. Disintegration comes about by the very causes that make the phenomenon; nothing further is needed. The factors that make it cause it to disintegrate.

Let us consider the first two moments of a table; this is a little complicated, but important to think through. At the time of the second moment of a table, its first moment has already disintegrated. The first moment has simply not remained. From this fact we can see that during the first moment the table is disintegrating; the first moment is not remaining; it is approaching not having remained. Thus the first moment itself has a nature of disintegrating.

What causes this disintegration? It does not take any causes beyond those that produce the table itself; those very causes create it with a nature of disintegration. This is the meaning of the statement that whatever is made by causes and conditions is necessarily impermanent. That is the first aphorism: All compounded things are impermanent. This means that whatever is created by the coming together of causes is momentary. By seeing that the true nature of things is disintegration, you will not be shocked by change when it occurs, not even death.

THE SECOND APHORISM

Reflecting on the moment-by-moment disintegration of things draws us to notice that people and things do not operate under their own power, independently. Firstly, phenomena depend for their very existence on the causes that produce them; secondly, their disintegration occurs without relying on any further causes. They are totally dependent on the causes and conditions that produce them; they are under the influence of something beyond themselves; they are not under their own power.

Since effects depend on their causes, favorable causes produce good effects, whereas unfavorable causes produce bad effects. If I may make a joke, this is not to say that bad parents necessarily have bad children, and good parents necessarily have good children! A plethora of causes and conditions are involved in who we turn out to be.

Our mind-body complex in this life was set up by actions, or karmas, in previous lives, and those actions were driven at least by ignorance of the true nature of phenomena but also by lust, hatred, and so forth that are rooted in ignorance. Thus our present life is not under its own power but is influenced by causes from the past, especially ignorance.

Ignorance itself has an unsalutary name; it indicates a lack of knowledge, but in this context it also refers to a twisted consciousness that mistakes the facts, and whatever is derived from it is miserable. Misery here refers not just to painful feeling but to the more general condition for the three levels of suffering mentioned earlier.

According to the Buddhist viewpoint, the external environment and the mind-body complex of beings living in the environ-ment are shaped by actions driven by ignorance. Any phenomenon under the influence of this ignorance has a nature of suffering. That is the second aphorism: All things contaminated by karmas rooted in destructive emotions are miserable.

THE THIRD APHORISM

The fact that something is created means that it relies on its re-spective causes, but things appear as though they exist under their own power. They appear in a false aspect. The mind-body com-plex seems to operate under its own power, but this is untrue. It is empty of that which it appears to be.

This conflict between appearance and reality indicates that suffering can be removed because it is based on a mistaken view of the way things are. Ignorance leads us to conclude that people have an independent existence, but this is not true. People and other phenomena are empty of such status. That is the third aphorism: All phenomena are selfless.

THE FOURTH APHORISM

When you understand that accepting things as existing the way they appear to be under their own power is simply wrong, you real-ize that perceiving phenomena to be empty of the way they seem to exist is valid and wise. Ignorance and wisdom are at odds, so when one increases in strength, the other weakens. In addition, because ignorance lacks a valid foundation, it can be removed through familiarization with wisdom. By generating wisdom we can put an end to the contamination of ignorance, and reach the peace of nirvana. That is the fourth aphorism: Nirvana is peace; it is ultimate happiness.

Contemplation

The four aphorisms, which all stem from the initial doctrine of subtle impermanence, have great impact. Consider this:

1. Things made by causes change moment by moment.
2. The causes of a phenomenon themselves make it have a nature of disintegration from the start.
3. Impermanent phenomena are totally under the influence of the causes and conditions that produce them.
4. Our present mind-body complex does not operate under its own power but under the influence of past causes, specifically ignorance. This indicates that it is under the sway of suffering.
5. That our mind-body complex appears to exist under its own power but does not underscores the conflict between its appearance and reality.
6. Wisdom calls for perceiving phenomena to be empty of the way they seem to exist; this is how it can oppose the mistakes made through the ignorant view that phenomena exist independently.
7. Thorough development of wisdom yields the peace of passing beyond suffering, yields nirvana.

THE MEASURE OF SUCCESS

After repeated meditation on the faults of cyclic existence that lead to lives revolving through birth, aging, sickness, and death, eventually you seek liberation from the depths of your heart, like a prisoner desperate to get out of a prison. No matter how difficult it might seem at first to generate such an attitude, with persistent effort it will come. As Shantideva says:

> There is nothing whatsoever that does not become easier
> When you have become accustomed to it.

In time, you will not be carried away by superficial thoughts like "Oh, I really must have this" or "This is truly terrific."

If your insight does not reach this level, but is merely verbal, it will not stir your mind from the depths. Your compassion also will not reach fullness. Having seen the problems of cyclic existence from many viewpoints, Bodhisattvas turn away from cyclic existence with a strong, single-pointed desire for liberation, but out of compassion they take rebirth so that they can help sentient beings. By abandoning any aspiration for themselves alone, they advance the well-being of others.

Let us now turn to considering this compassionate level of spiritual practice.

HIGH LEVEL OF
PRACTICE

14

Altruism

Altruism is a source of goodness for yourself and others,
Medicine alleviating all troubles,
The great path traveled by the wise,
Nourishment for all who see, hear, remember, and
    contact it,
Possessing great efficacy for advancing others' welfare.
Through it you indirectly achieve your own interests in
    full.

—TSONGKHAPA, *GREAT*
    TREATISE ON THE STAGES OF
    THE PATH

The main reason why Shakyamuni Buddha, who lived over 2,500 years ago, is still identified as an exemplary being is the fact that he was strongly influenced by great compassion. His commitment to altruism was not limited to a few acts of kindness or to a short period of time; he single-pointedly practiced great compassion for countless eons in lifetime after lifetime. This concern for others, together with fully developed wisdom, led him to become free from all defects, endowed with all the fine qualities of an enlightened teacher, renowned to this day.

It is also clear that the fame of other great teachers with great followings, such as Moses, Jesus, and Mohammed, arose from the power of altruism. Throughout history the people whose lives truly inspire us are those who devoted themselves to helping others. We admire them and take pleasure in reading about them. Biographies of those who harm others generate fear and dislike when they are read or even considered. Both types of biographies are about people, but the difference lies in their attitude, in their intentions to help or to harm. Indeed, when we look with an unbiased mind at the life stories of prominent people over the past three thousand years, the favorable ones are motivated by altruism, whereas the opposite ones sought to harm others.

When we spend time with someone who looks nice but is not so nice inside, our initial response changes; conversely when someone is not so attractive externally but has an appealing attitude, we find ourselves thinking, "This person is really nice." The beauty of our internal attitude is most important. Even animals like someone with a good outlook. I doubt that animals judge people by their external beauty; they sense the inner disposition, whether the being is sympathetic or harmful. In this respect animals are perhaps more reliable, whereas humans, by considering temporary gain, can be more devious and more easily duped.

My point is that if we want others to be nice to us, we should have a good attitude toward them. Humans spend a huge amount of money making their bodies beautiful, and in comparison spend little on making their minds appealing. Others can make your body beautiful, but only you can make your mind beautiful.

ALTRUISM ALSO HELPS ONESELF

As Tsongkhapa repeatedly says, "Working at achieving others' welfare accomplishes your own along the way." It is a profound truth that insofar as you are devoted to others' benefit, that is the measure by which you yourself will benefit. Many value altruism and even praise it, but do not see its relevance to their own well-being. Some even think that strong devotion to the concerns of others would undermine their own benefit because it would require neglecting their own welfare. However, what needs to be stopped is not concern for your own development but excessive self-cherishing, in which your entire focus of attention rests on yourself. This is the switch from self-cherishing to other-cherishing that is called for in Buddhist texts.

If the foolishness of self-cherishing is not set aside and the transformative attitude of cherishing others is not adopted, we will not find any comfort in this world, much less attain the supremely altruistic state of Buddhahood. As Shantideva says:

If you do not switch your concern
From your own happiness to relieving others' pain,
Not only will you not achieve Buddhahood,
There will be no pleasures while in cyclic existence.

INTERRELATIONSHIP

The essence of human society is interdependence. No matter how powerful a single individual may be, it is impossible for that person to be successful all alone. Humans have a social nature and therefore must depend on each other. Lust fails at the task of drawing together what is favorable even to ourselves because at its core it is biased. In lust what seems to be affection for another is prejudiced, so even the slightest interference lets hatred set in. Altruism, however, is supremely effective at drawing beneficial factors together because its unbiased nature will never push us to do irrational harm. Altruism is endowed only with good qualities.

We have to act to remain alive; without taking action we would die. When our actions in any field of endeavor are relevant to the true situation, they can achieve the desired result. Consider what is required to make a meal (though indeed I must admit I do not know how to cook!). It does not help just to want to make a good meal without knowing what sorts of vegetables to use and how to cut and cook them. By knowing what is needed, you can make good food. Similarly, it is crucial to know the real situation when engaging in any action.

What is the actual situation? The happiness that we want depends on many causes and conditions, as does the suffering we seek to avoid. This being the case, the true status of happiness and suffering can be realized only from a broad outlook; it cannot be seen from a narrow perspective. Neither the attainment of happiness nor the avoidance of pain can be achieved by just looking at a single factor.

With lust and hatred, your outlook is necessarily constricted, limited to a confined target. For example, when you become angry at a painful situation, you do not see the web of contributing conditions, whereas if you saw the full extent of the contributing factors, hatred would be impossible. By focusing on just one particular factor among the many giving rise to a problem, you close the door to open-mindedness and thereby to your own happiness.

Afflictive emotions require a fixed target, seemingly real and true, self-existent, and autonomous. When destructive emotions take the scene, it becomes all the harder to see that the situation is dependent on a multitude of interrelated circumstances, whereas in the absence of lust and hatred this is much easier to see.

All of us can appreciate that altruism, on the other hand, is a nonafflictive attitude; by its very nature it is broad-minded, which allows us to easily consider a broad array of interdependent factors. Whether in economics, politics, commerce, science, culture, social welfare, or any type of activity, nothing happens based just on a single condition. Since the truth is always embedded in a vast network of conditions, the broader your outlook is, the greater the possibility of success at constructing something positive or undoing something negative.

When we attempt to fix a problem without this broad outlook, we create a lot of trouble for ourselves and others. Many of the predicaments that we see in the world today are due to not seeing the greater picture but concentrating on just one facet, targeting, for instance, a single person as the source of problems, thinking "This is my enemy." Focusing only on your self-interest is the problem; being concerned for others is the solution.

I often say to those whom I meet that although a thorough explanation of the view of dependent-arising is found in Buddhism, it is not merely Buddhist. It is critical in many situations throughout our world. This perspective of interconnectedness is relevant in myriad fields because it provides a holistic outlook. Altruism is the door for opening up this broad view.

ALTRUISM BRINGS COURAGE

Concern for others also gives you courage. When you are solely concerned with "I," this naturally leads to fear and anxiety, resulting in even more insecurity, making the body imbalanced and riddled with health problems. However, deep within altruism lies courage, which diminishes fear and bestows relaxation, which in turn has beneficial effects on blood pressure and overall well-being.

Recently, when I attended a meeting with scientists in New York, a doctor reported that people who repeatedly use the word *I* are more likely to suffer from heart disease. He did not cite the reason, but it seems to me that putting "I" at the center makes a person's perspective restricted and uptight, which cannot be good for the heart. However, when concern for others is paramount, this provides a broad openness that makes a great difference. If I were a doctor, I would probably write in all my prescriptions to patients, "Be altruistic, and you will get better!"

Each of us has been born into this world, and each of us has been provided with a way to help others. A kind attitude of concern for those in our respective field of activity will affect them, even if it is just ten people, bringing them more comfort and less strife. If each of them, in turn, treats their associates in a similar way, then even though the effect will be gradual, it will in time be transformative. This is how we can change the world.

BECOMING A PRACTITIONER
OF GREAT CAPACITY

The way to rise to a higher level of spiritual practice is to develop altruism to the point where seeking enlightenment in order to serve others more effectively becomes your inner, spontaneous motivation. This other-directed aspiration to enlightenment becomes the ultimate form of altruism when it works together with the wisdom of dependent-arising. This is why in this final section of the book we will focus on how to deepen compassion and how to develop wisdom.

Buddha himself practiced the altruistic intention to become enlightened from the time of his original inspiration, and his ultimate advice to followers was to internalize this intention to cherish others more than themselves. I myself feel fortunate to be teaching how to do this in accordance with his thoughts, as well as those of such great Indian scholar-practitioners as Nagarjuna, and I hope that you too feel fortunate to be reading about it. An oral transmission in Tibet relates the story of a teacher in the late seventeenth century who was devoted to this practice. One day, after explaining this topic, he said, "Today I had the opportunity to explain about love, compassion, and the altruistic intention to become enlightened, and I feel so refreshed!"

Contemplation

Consider:

1. We like life stories motivated by altruism, whereas hearing about the lives of those whose actions stemmed from wanting to harm others evokes fear and apprehension.

2. A beautiful internal attitude is more important than external beauty.

3. Only you can make your mind beautiful.

4. Working at achieving the welfare of others accomplishes your own along the way.

5. What needs to be stopped is not concern for your own development but self-cherishing in which almost the entire focus of attention is on yourself.

6. Lust fails to draw together what is favorable to ourselves because at its core it is biased and therefore stupid. In lust what seems to be affection for another is prejudiced, which allows hatred to set in upon even slight interference.

7. Altruism is supremely effective at drawing beneficial factors together because it is in accord with the very nature of interdependence, which lies at the heart of social interaction.

8. True happiness and freedom from suffering can be realized only from a broad outlook; it cannot be seen from a narrow perspective.

9. With lust and hatred, your outlook is necessarily constricted. By focusing on just one particular factor among the many giving rise to a problem, you close the door to broadmindedness.

10. Afflictive emotions require a seemingly real and autonomous target.

11. The broader your outlook is, the greater the possibility of constructing something positive or undoing something negative.

12. Focusing only on yourself is the problem; being concerned for others is the solution.

13. Understanding interdependence is relevant in myriad fields because it provides a holistic outlook. Altruism is the door for opening up this broad view.

14. When you are solely concerned with "I," this naturally leads to fear and anxiety, resulting in even more insecurity, making even the body imbalanced.

15. The world can be transformed as each of us changes our attitude; this change will spread from person to person.

16. The way to rise to a higher level of spiritual practice is to develop altruism to the point where seeking enlightenment in order to serve others more effectively becomes your inner, spontaneous motivation for everything you do.

15

Engendering
Great Compassion

The altruistic stay for a limitless time in the world.
For limitless beings they seek
The limitless qualities of enlightenment
And perform limitless virtuous actions.

—NAGARJUNA,

PRECIOUS GARLAND

OF ADVICE

Buddhists call an other-oriented outlook "great" because it aims at helping a limitless number of beings, whereas seeking to take care of yourself alone would be trifling. Since sentient beings have limitlessly different dispositions and interests, helping them calls for limitless teachings or other activities appropriate to their state. In addition, since there cannot be any consideration of the length of time required to help others, this calls for a limitless commitment to establish limitless beings in the limitless qualities of enlightenment.

Such an altruistic attitude is indeed amazing. Buddha said:

If whatever merit there is in the altruistic intention
To become enlightened had form,
It would fill the entire expanse of the sky
And then exceed it.

The presence of this other-directed attitude in your consciousness makes you a Bodhisattva, a hero (*sattva*) contemplating enlightenment (*bodhi*) for the sake of others. A lama by the name of Toyon described his attitude this way:

> May the virtuous roots that I have achieved through putting together this book have the result that instead of my ever achieving Buddhahood I remain in cyclic existence as long as space exists, experiencing the sufferings of other beings in place of them.

There are two methods for engendering such courageous altruism. One of these involves a set of seven cause-and-effect instructions, and the other a practice of switching self and other, which I will explain in this chapter and the next.

FOUNDATIONAL STEP: FREEING YOUR RELATIONSHIPS FROM BIAS

The seven cause-and-effect instructions begin with a practice that is not counted among the seven since it is the floor of practice. This foundation is the practice of equanimity, an even-mindedness toward others. To develop a profoundly vast commitment to others, it is necessary first to smooth out your attitude toward others, making it impartial. As Tsongkhapa says:

If you do not eliminate the bias of being attached to some and being hostile to others, any love or compassion you generate will be biased.

At present we feel a sense of intimacy, a closeness of heart, for our friends, which makes it easier for us to wish that they be freed from suffering and gain happiness. We turn away from our enemies, dismissing them or even taking pleasure in their misfortune. Toward those who are neither friend nor enemy we feel indifferent, neither attracted or repulsed. As Tsongkhapa starkly puts it:

> At present you find it unbearable that your friends suffer, but you are pleased that your enemies suffer, and you are indifferent to the suffering of neutral persons.

Ordinary sympathy for friends can even be an obstacle to generating compassion for all sentient beings because it is biased. Our usual sympathy is usually mixed with attachment, which therefore is mixed with an afflictive emotion. True compassion, on the other hand, comes from appreciating that the aspiration of others to enjoy happiness and avoid suffering is the same as your own, giving rise to a sympathetic wish that they too be free from suffering. Being based on reason, such compassion is not affected by whether the other person is a helpful friend or a harmful enemy, or just plain neutral. Real compassion does not depend on whether the other person is nice to you.

Ordinary affection has yourself as its basis, because you are responding to another's being nice to you. Ordinary sympathy, our usual intimacy, is therefore biased, whereas real compassion has others as its basis.

Transforming Reactions

Developing equanimity is not a matter of telling yourself that you do not have friends and enemies, for there is no denying that someone who helps is a friend, and someone who harms is an enemy. However, since over the course of time things change, friends and enemies should not be fixed categories. What you are trying to accomplish is to stop reacting to some people with attachment simply because at the moment they are friends, and stop reacting to others with hostility simply because right now they happen to be enemies. As Tsongkhapa says:

> It is not the notion of friend or enemy that you need to stop but the bias that comes from attachment and hostility, which are based on the reason that some people are your friends and others your enemies.

By developing equanimity you seek to stop using the fact that someone is harming you or your friends as a reason for being hostile to that person. Instead, as Shantideva says, you should take this same fact and use it as a reason for practicing patience toward that person. After all, an enemy is a supreme opportunity for generating the important practice of compassionate forbearance, and thus is as valuable as a spiritual guide.

Contemplation

1. Imagine a friend, an enemy, and a neutral person standing before you.
2. With one part of your mind consider your attitudes toward your enemy, your friend, and the neutral person.

3. Does your enemy appear to be completely unattractive, having harmed you or your friends in this life?

4. Does your friend appear to be completely attractive, having helped you or your intimates in this life?

5. Does the neutral person appear to be neither of these?

6. Consider that over the course of many lifetimes and even within this present lifetime there is no certainty at all that an enemy will remain an enemy, a friend will remain a friend, or that a neutral person will remain neutral.

7. Decide that therefore it is not right to single out just one group for intimacy, another just for indifference, and yet another solely for alienation.

8. Consider that all beings are the same; they want happiness and not suffering, just as you do.

Reflecting this way will remove bias.

FIRST STEP: FINDING EVERYONE DEAR

Once you have developed a basic attitude of even-mindedness toward others, the next step in engendering compassion is to find a perspective through which you can view everyone as being appealing in some respect. This is obviously not easy, but:

- Since consciousness, as mentioned earlier, has to be produced from consciousness, its continuum has to be beginningless.
- Once we establish that the continuum of your mind has no beginning, the person that depends upon that continuum of consciousness also cannot have a beginning.

- Once the person, or "I," has no beginning, you must have taken rebirth over and over.
- Hence in the cyclic existence of birth and death you may have been born in any place with any type of body.
- The bodies assumed in those births must have included various types, those born from a womb and birth from an egg.
- Most births from a womb or from an egg require a nurturer, someone to look after the newborn.
- Thus there is no saying that any particular being has not taken care of you in the past or will not do so in the future.

Buddhists call this reflection "recognizing all sentient beings as mothers," but the model does not have to be your mother; it can be any nurturing being. Buddha said:

I have difficulty seeing a place where you have not been born, traversed, or died in the long past. I have difficulty seeing any person in the long past who has not been your father, mother, uncle, aunt, sister, master, abbot, guru, or guiding figure.

In this way you can come to see that there is no being who has not nurtured you, or helped you, in an intimate way.

Contemplation

Consider:

1. Once it becomes clear that consciousness has to be produced from a cause of similar type, the continuum of your mind has to be beginningless.
2. Once you see that the continuum of your mind has no beginning, the person that is founded in dependence upon

that continuum of consciousness also could have no beginning.

3. Once the person, or "I," has no beginning, you must have
taken rebirth over and over.

4. Hence there is no saying that in the cyclic existence of birth
and death you did not take rebirth in any particular place or
with any particular type of body.

5. The bodies assumed in those births must have been of various types, including birth from a womb (human and animal)
and birth from an egg (birds and so forth).

6. Most births from a womb or from an egg require a nurturer,
someone to look after you.

7. There is no saying that any particular being has not taken
care of you and will not do so again in the future.

8. In this fundamental sense everyone is close to you, intimate.

SECOND STEP: BEING AWARE
OF HOW EVERYONE HELPED

The next phase in the development of compassion is to intensify
this sense of intimacy by reflecting on everyone's kindness when
they nurtured you. Bring to mind the ways your mother or another
nurturer sustained you with kindness during the early part of your
present life. Consider how much affection birds and mammals show
their young. It is indeed amazing; even most insects do the same.

Since most newborn animals require care and nurturing for
weeks, months, and sometimes even years, affection naturally de-
velops between the nurtured and the nurturer. Animals that suckle
at the breast have a sense of intimacy and affection for the mother,
and the mother also has those feelings for her offspring. Without

such affection she would not take care of the child. Biology itself calls for togetherness.

Still, there are some animals, such as turtles and butterflies, that do not form this kind of relationship between mother and child. The mother lays her eggs and leaves; the child has to take care of itself. Given that this is their nature, it seems to me that even if mother turtle and child turtle were later brought together, they would have no special affection for each other.

What I am referring to is not spiritual but simply biology. Beings who depend on one another naturally develop a sense of affection. Since humans must rely on another early in life, affection definitely has to form between the mother and child. Tsongkhapa describes this relationship as follows:

> As your mother, she protected you from all harm and provided you all benefit and happiness. In particular, in this lifetime she nurtured you tirelessly in various ways: She carried you for a long time in her womb; then, when you were a helpless, newborn infant, she held you to the warmth of her flesh and rocked you back and forth on the tips of her ten fingers; she suckled you at her breast, gave you soft food, wiped your nose, and cleared away your excrement.
>
> When you were hungry and thirsty, she gave you food and drink; when you were cold, clothes; when you had nothing, everything of value. If you suffered from illness, pain, or the threat of death, your mother made the choice from the depths of her heart that she would rather be sick than you be sick, she would rather be in pain than you be in pain, she would rather die than you die. By putting this feeling into action, she did what was needed to alleviate these troubles for you.

Tsongkhapa's intimate description calls us to remember and to imagine how family members and best friends have cared for us through countless lifetimes.

In many Tibetan prayers we make salutary wishes for "all mother sentient beings." Because such teachings are widespread in Tibet, from childhood we became accustomed to such phrases, providing us with a model of how to view others and enkindle a kind attitude toward others. This helps us so that when we are introduced to teachings about love, compassion, and the altruistic intention to become enlightened, we put effort into implementing them. This is a strength of Tibetan culture.

Contemplation

1. Call to mind the many ways, whether animal or human, that a mother or other caregiver nurtures the child.
2. Consider how, whether born as an animal or a human, a child puts hope in and generates affection for the nurturer.
3. Reflect on this situation until feeling stirs in you.
4. Realize that at some time over the course of countless lifetimes your friends have nurtured you in this way, and acknowledge their kindness.
5. Realize that at some time over the course of lifetimes neutral persons have nurtured you in this way, and acknowledge their kindness.
6. Realize that at some time over the course of lifetimes your enemies have nurtured you in this way, and acknowledge their kindness.

In this way you will gradually become mindful of the intimate kindnesses that all beings have extended to you.

THIRD STEP: RECIPROCATING THE KINDNESS OF OTHERS

All these sentient beings, who may have kindly provided for you over the course of lifetimes, undergo physical and mental pain. Even when outright pain is not present, they are weighed down with having performed deeds that will bring about suffering in the future and are presently headed in the direction of actions that will result in more pain. Since it is a general custom throughout the world to reciprocate kindness and to consider those who do not do so to be boorish, how could it be suitable for someone who is a follower of Buddha and intent on internalizing the high level of Buddhist practices to ignore those who have, without beginning, nurtured you out of kindness?

How to Respond in Return

Responding to this kindness by providing sentient beings with temporary assistance, though helpful, is not sufficient, since it will not last. Even if you help someone to achieve a good lifetime next time around, it will only be one of many. Rather than only offering temporary support, the best assistance is to help them achieve the stable, lasting peace of liberation from cyclic existence and the full physical and mental perfection of Buddhahood. Tsongkhapa paints a vivid picture of the proper attitude of reciprocation:

> Imagine that your mother is crazed, unable to remain composed. She is blind, has no guide, and stumbles with every step as she approaches a frightful precipice. If she cannot place hope in her child for help, in whom can she put trust? If her

child does not take responsibility for freeing her from this terror, who would take responsibility? Her child must set her free.

In the same way, the madness of afflictive emotions disturbs the peace of mind of living beings, your mothers. Having no control over their minds, they are crazed; they lack eyes to see the way to a favorable rebirth and to the definite goodness of liberation and omniscience. They have no true teacher, a guide for the blind. They stumble from their wrongdoing crippling them each moment. When these motherly beings see the edge of the precipice of cyclic existence in general and the miserable realms in particular, they naturally put hope in their children, and their children naturally have a responsibility to get their mothers out of this situation. With this in mind, return your mothers' kindness by definitely causing them to be relieved from cyclic existence.

Although in general one should not emphasize others' deficiencies, in the context of this meditation you are focusing on the miserable plight of those who nurture us. You need to train in an intention to return their kindness from within realistically assessing their situation.

Contemplation

Consider:

1. All the motherly sentient beings who have kindly provided for you over the course of lifetimes undergo physical and mental pain.
2. Also, they are weighed down by having performed deeds that will create future suffering.

3. In addition, they are presently headed in the direction of actions that will result in more pain.

4. It would be vulgar not to return their kindness.

5. The best reciprocation would be to help them achieve the stable, lasting peace and bliss of liberation from cyclic existence and the full physical and mental perfection of Buddhahood.

6. Imagine:

> Your mother is crazed, blind, guideless, stumbling with every step as she nears a cliff. If she cannot place hope in her child for help, in whom can she put trust? If her child does not take responsibility for freeing her from this terror, who would take responsibility? Her child must set her free. In the same way, the madness of afflictive emotions disturbs the peace of mind of living beings, your nurturers. Having no control over their minds, they are crazed; they lack eyes to see the way to a favorable rebirth and to the definite goodness of liberation and omniscience. They have no true teacher, a guide for the blind. They stumble from their wrongdoing, which cripples them each moment. When these motherly beings see the edge of the precipice of cyclic existence in general and the miserable realms in particular, they naturally put hope in their children, and their children naturally have a responsibility to get their mothers out of this situation.

With this in mind, train in the intention to reciprocate the kindness of your infinite mothers by helping them achieve release from suffering and limitation.

FOURTH STEP: CULTIVATING LOVE

The Buddha defeated hosts of evil with the power of love.
Hence, love is the supreme protector.
— TSONGKHAPA

By having cultivated the previous meditations (even-mindedness, seeing everyone as a nurturer, becoming mindful of how they helped you, and developing an intention to reciprocate their kindness) you have developed a sense of intimacy with all beings and a wish to help them. In the next step you cultivate love.

There are three levels of love to be cultivated toward the three groups identified earlier: your friends, neutral beings, and finally enemies. Imagining a friend in front of you, meditate on each of these levels of love until you feel it deeply:

1. This person wants happiness but is deprived. *How nice it would be* if she or he could be imbued with happiness and all of its causes!

2. This person wants happiness but is deprived. *May* she or he be imbued with happiness and all its causes.

3. This person wants happiness but is deprived. *I will do whatever I can* to help her or him to be imbued with happiness and all the causes of happiness!

Make sure to start with individual beings from these groups, and then extend this loving attitude gradually to more and more until it can cover all sentient beings. As Tsongkhapa says:

If you train in these attitudes of impartiality, love, and compassion without using specific objects of meditation, but only using a general object such as "all beings" from the outset, you will just *seem* to generate these attitudes, and when you try to apply them to specific individuals, you will not be able to actually generate them toward anyone. Therefore, once you have transformative experience toward an individual in your meditation practice, then gradually increase the number of individuals you consider. Finally, take all beings in general as your object of meditation.

The value of proceeding this way with individual beings—first friends, and then neutral beings, and finally enemies—is incalculable.

Contemplation

1. Imagine your best friend in front of you and meditate on each of the three strengths of love until you deeply feel it:
   — This person wants happiness but is deprived. *How nice it would be* if she or he could be imbued with happiness and all of its causes!
   — This person wants happiness but is deprived. *May* she or he be imbued with happiness and all its causes.
   — This person wants happiness but is deprived. *I will do whatever I can* to help her or him to be imbued with happiness and all the causes of happiness!
2. Extend this meditation to more friends, one by one.
3. Imagine a neutral person in front of you and meditate on each of the three strengths of love until you deeply feel it:

— This person wants happiness but is deprived. *How nice it would be* if she or he could be imbued with happiness and all of its causes!

— This person wants happiness but is deprived. *May* she or he be imbued with happiness and all its causes.

— This person wants happiness but is deprived. *I will do whatever I can* to help her or him to be imbued with happiness and all the causes of happiness!

4. Extend this meditation to more neutral persons, one by one.

5. Imagine your least enemy in front of you and meditate on each of three strengths of love until you deeply feel it:

— This person wants happiness but is deprived. *How nice it would be* if she or he could be imbued with happiness and all of its causes!

— This person wants happiness but is deprived. *May* she or he be imbued with happiness and all its causes.

— This person wants happiness but is deprived. *I will do whatever I can* to help her or him to be imbued with happiness and all the causes of happiness!

6. Extend this meditation to more enemies, one by one.

Considering the Destitute

When cultivating love, another technique is to bring to mind sentient beings who are destitute, such as the poor and vulnerable. When we hear the news, we constantly learn about beings in awful situations such as famine, flood, and extreme poverty. They are all like ourselves in wanting happiness, but due to many external and internal circumstances they find themselves in dire straits.

It is important that when beings in such situations come to your attention, you cultivate love toward them, thinking, "What an awful situation! May they have happiness!" If you think this way from time to time when watching the news on television or reading the newspaper, it helps cultivate love toward all sentient beings.

It might cross your mind, "Why bother to think about all of this? It's better just to stay in my own comfort zone." However, as I mentioned earlier, when you help others, you yourself benefit in equal measure. This will be confirmed by your own experience in this lifetime; when your own problems no longer dominate your mind, you will see improvements in physical health, openness of outlook, and peace of mind. Also, over the course of future lifetimes the effects of this practice will continue to bring comfort.

Contemplation

When watching the news or reading the newspaper about beings in awful situations such as famine, flood, and extreme poverty, consider:

1. These beings are all like myself in wanting happiness and in having the right to gain happiness, but due to external and internal circumstances they find themselves in dire straits.
2. Think, "What an awful situation! May they have happiness!"

FIFTH STEP: COMPASSION

When cultivating compassion, consider the terrible situation that so many are in. Take to heart how countless numbers of defenseless animals are exploited by humans. Turn your attention toward the excessive slaughter of animals. When we eat meat, we make remarks such as "This meat is tasty," "This meat is not delicious," but, in fact, the meat we eat is the body of a sentient being, and we do not have a right to it. Humans are excessively greedy. The vast numbers of chicken farms, pig farms, and fish farms need to be reconsidered. In the past people throughout the world more or less took care of themselves. They killed animals but not on our current scale. For the sake of accumulating more wealth, today huge enterprises have been established for exploiting animals. When you think about how these animals suffer, there is no way to avoid making them the objects of love and compassion.

In the past there was no such thing as a mega chicken farm, but nowadays under the sway of economic development there are huge chicken-raising enterprises in the wealthier countries, and almost all restaurants offer chicken. Consider the conditions in those huge chicken houses, how those animals suffer, how much fear they have, and how vulnerable they are. It will stir your heart until it is hard to bear.

Think about such situations for other animals such as sheep, cows, yaks, and pigs and, of course, humans as well. They all want to be rid of pain and have the right to do so, but they suffer from unwanted sufferings one after another. Think about their endless pain, and raise up the wish that they be free from it. Train this way.

Considering Evildoers

Also, take to mind beings who are engaged in obviously evil actions. Whether they are currently undergoing outright pain or not, through their actions they are causing themselves pain in the future, and thus they should also be objects of compassion.

Considering Persons Corrupted by Power

If during the middle level of practice you successfully identified the three types of suffering (outright mental and physical pain, the suffering of change, and the suffering of pervasive conditioning) in terms of your own life, you can readily understand that many people corrupted by power harbor mistaken notions that worldly pleasures are true happiness. (As explained above, these are actually instances of the sufferings of change.) They are under the very strong influence of afflictive ideas; they are dominated by ignorance.

If you have successfully identified your own suffering of pervasive conditioning, you can also readily understand that all those seemingly mighty persons are also beset by the suffering of pervasive conditioning, wrapped in the influence of afflictive emotions, deprived of being under their own power, and beset by self-destruction. You will think:

> No matter who looks into it, it can be seen that these misguided, though powerful, people are under the influence of counterproductive attitudes, doing the work of self-destruction. What a mess they are in! If they could only be free from suffering and the causes of suffering, how nice it would be!

Considering Winning and Losing

In a situation in which someone is being pushed around by another, we pity the one who is losing out and we are upset with the aggressor. We see the suffering of the loser, but we pay no attention to the greater pain that the aggressor will endure in the future from accumulating the karma of perpetrating such a vile action.

The loser is undergoing the fruit of a bad action performed earlier and will not have to experience it again, whereas the aggressor is accumulating a new karma that will cause him or her to experience over many lives the suffering that is the fruit of this awful deed. From this viewpoint, we should have greater compassion for the perpetrator.

The ability to think this way opens the door to the practice of patience. For example, if someone harms you, you will reflect that you are experiencing the effects of an earlier unfortunate action and thereby are being cleansed of that karma, but your attacker is accumulating a new bad karma that has yet to yield its bitter fruit. From this viewpoint, you can take pity on the aggressor; instead of getting angry at the person harming you, you will feel compassion, opening the way for easily generating patience, forbearance, tolerance.

Contemplation

As with love, compassion is to be cultivated first toward your friends, then neutral beings, and finally enemies. Meditate on each of the three increasing strengths of compassion until you deeply feel it.

1. Imagine your best friend in front of you and meditate as follows:

    — This person wants happiness and not suffering, yet is stricken with outright physical and mental pain, the pain of change, and the pain of pervasive conditioning. *How nice it would be* if he or she could only be free from suffering and the causes of suffering!

    — This person wants happiness and not suffering, yet is stricken with outright physical and mental pain, the pain of change, and the pain of pervasive conditioning. *May he or she be free from suffering and the causes of suffering!*

— This person wants happiness and not suffering, yet is stricken with outright physical and mental pain, the pain of change, and the pain of pervasive conditioning. *I will do whatever I can* to help him or her be free from suffering and the causes of suffering!

2. Extend this meditation to more friends, one by one.

3. Imagine a neutral person in front of you and meditate on each of the three strengths of compassion until you feel it deeply.

4. Extend this meditation to more neutral persons, one by one.

5. Imagine your least enemy in front of you and meditate on each of the three strengths of compassion until you deeply feel it.

6. Extend this meditation to more enemies, one by one.

Gradual Practice

As you keep working at developing compassion day by day, in time you will arrive at a point when you have strong sympathy and empathy for all sentient beings. This marks the attainment of great compassion. Kamalashila's *Stages of Meditation* says:

> When you spontaneously feel compassion wishing to completely eliminate the sufferings of all living beings—just like a mother's wish to relieve her dear, sweet child's sickness—then your compassion is complete and is therefore called great compassion.

Since forces of misguided selfishness are embedded in our minds, keep up this practice both in meditation and during daily activities. As Tsongkhapa says:

> Your mind stream has been infused since beginningless time with the bitter taste of the afflictive emotions, so it will not change from just short cultivation of love, compassion, and the like. Therefore, sustain meditation continuously.

SIXTH STEP: TOTAL COMMITMENT

In the penultimate step you take upon yourself the responsibility of bringing help and happiness to all sentient beings. For this, it is not sufficient to wish that all beings be endowed with happiness and the causes of happiness and be freed from suffering and the causes of suffering. Now you need to take on the burden of the well-being of others by resolving that you will provide help and happiness to all living beings even if you have to accomplish this alone.

Contemplation

To develop this supreme altruistic will:

1. Take to mind again and again the meaning of this stanza from Shantideva's *A Guide to the Bodhisattva's Way of Life*:
   As long as space remains and there are
   transmigrating beings,
   May I remain relieving the sufferings of sentient
   beings.

2. Remember to dedicate all your virtuous activities and the beneficial karmas established in your mind stream to the benefit of all sentient beings.

3. Resolve:

> Even if I have to do it alone, I will free all sentient beings from suffering and the causes of suffering, and connect all sentient beings with happiness and its causes.

As you gradually develop familiarity with these contemplations, you will feel their impact.

SEVENTH STEP: ASPIRING TO ENLIGHTENMENT

Now that you have a strong resolve to help others, when you analyze whether you have the capacity to actually help others, you realize that in order to be effective you must attain your own perfection in body, speech, and mind. This is accomplished by achieving the enlightenment of a Buddha so that you can thoroughly know others' dispositions and also know what techniques to teach them. You must become enlightened in order to most effectively benefit others.

When this double aspiration (to help others and to attain your own enlightenment in order to be of highest service) becomes as strong outside of meditation as it is in meditation, you have generated the altruistic intention to become enlightened, and have become a Bodhisattva (a hero intending to achieve enlightenment).

Contemplation

1. Analyze whether at present you have the capacity to help others become endowed with happiness and free from suffering.

2. Consider that in addition to providing temporary help it is necessary to educate beings so that they themselves can become enlightened.

3. Draw the conclusion that you must achieve enlightenment in order to remove the obstacles to knowing others' interests and dispositions, and to knowing which particular techniques are needed to help them.

4. Resolve to achieve enlightenment in order to help others to the fullest.

16

Switching Self and Other

Whatever joy there is in the world
Arises from wishing for others' happiness.
Whatever suffering there is in the world
Arises from wishing for your own happiness.

—SHANTIDEVA

Now we turn to the other method of engendering concern for others, called "switching self and other." What needs to be stopped is not concern for your own development but excessive self-cherishing, in which almost the entire focus of attention is just on yourself. We begin by considering how everyone has provided us with assistance.

HOW EVERYONE HAS HELPED YOU

As was explained in the previous chapter, everyone has at certain times been your nurturer over the course of countless lifetimes. In addition to this, all sentient beings throughout limitless space have directly or indirectly provided services that have benefitted you; regardless of their motivation they have been kind to you. For instance, your food, clothing, residence, friendship, reputation, and accessories such as cameras and watches all come by way of other sentient beings.

What you eat arrives on your plate thanks to others; farmers work in the fields even when it rains, whereas most of us can take refuge inside a building. Also, they have to kill a great many insects and bugs. Our cotton clothing comes from others who have planted cotton, cultivated it, and picked it; even when much of this work is done by machine, it takes a lot of hard work. Consider silk cloth and brocade; think of all the silk worms that have to be killed. Look at leather jackets and fur coats; they may be worn as adornments, but they all come from killing animals. And pearl jewelry; think of how many oysters have to be killed!

Our homes are created by hard-working builders; as soon as they finish a house, they have to leave for another worksite. We move in and then criticize this feature or that one. Look at the difficult lives of coolies; they are for the most part stuck in that kind of life.

Consider even a shoe box, made with care but discarded when we get our new shoes home, though indeed some of us make good use of them. All of these things exist thanks to others.

Friendship is dependent on others. You cannot have companionship alone. Humans need affection, right? It is comforting when another being shows us affection. A sentient being is needed for that. Even a cat or dog knows how to do this, but a diamond cannot, no matter how expensive it is. I doubt that a flea could show affection to us, but most animals can respond to our showing affection to them. Companionship is dependent on other living beings, and it is very valuable.

You cannot have fame if you are alone. It requires that others spread the word about you.

All of these things, whether born of a motivation to help you or not, provide a valuable service, and thus we should value them. My watch has no affection for me, but because it helps me, I appreciate it, even cherish it, and keep it from hitting against anything else. Also, as Shantideva says, we value the end of suffering even though, not having any thought, the cessation of suffering does not have any affection for us. But because it can help us we appreciate it, and value the spiritual practices that bring it about. My point is that appreciation and valuing do not necessarily depend on the motivation to help.

Our human life itself comes from moral actions in previous lives; similarly, long life, freedom from illness, being endowed with resources, creditable speech, and strength all come from moral actions in former lives (like saving another's life or donating food). Most of these actions are performed in relation to others. Attainment of a good life next time around is possible due to other sentient beings, as is the attainment of liberation from cyclic existence. Even though the wisdom realizing selflessness and the development of a concentrated meditation do not depend on others, the practice of morality, which is their very foundation, must take place in relation to others because morality is based on not harming others; without other sentient beings you cannot perform the virtuous deeds that stop harming them. For example, the virtue of abandoning killing requires others, as does abandoning stealing, sexual misconduct, and most other virtues. Without others, these virtues which are productive of positive results could not be practiced.

It goes without saying that attainment of Buddhahood relies on others, since the distinctive practices for achieving that state are love, compassion, and the altruistic intention to become enlightened, which come from being aware of the suffering of others and being moved from the depths of your heart to bring help and happiness to them. We should respect those who suffer as much as we respect the Buddha; as Shantideva says:

> Living beings and the Buddha are similar
> Since from them you achieve a Buddha's qualities.
> How is it that you do not respect living beings
> Just as you respect the Buddha?

In this way we come to see that whether others have benefitted you intentionally or not, they have assisted you either directly or indirectly.

Enemies are particularly valuable for those cultivating love and compassion. What destroys love and compassion is anger, and what undermines anger is patience, which cannot be practiced without an enemy. Enemies provide a valuable opportunity for practicing patience, so from that viewpoint they are very valuable. Thus it becomes clear that all sentient beings throughout space have directly or indirectly benefited you, even during your present lifetime.

You might protest that the cessation of suffering has no motivation to harm and thus is valued, whereas an enemy wishes to harm, and so is not comparable. However, doctors who might have to bring us pain in the course of treatment that is motivated to help do not provide us with a chance to cultivate patience, but an enemy who harms us out of desire to do so does give us that chance.

In this case the presence of a motivation to harm is more valuable than its opposite; we might even say, more kind.

HOW EVERYONE IS SIMILAR

Consider too how we are all similar. Shantideva says:

Impermanent yourself,
Toward which impermanent being
Will you have lust?
Impermanent yourself,
Toward which impermanent being
Will you have hate?

There is no reason for considering yourself worthwhile and neglecting everyone else. Both you and others are equally stuck in cyclic existence with the burden of a mind-body system that was born of destructive emotions and karma. Both you and others are approaching death under the looming influence of impermanence.

Consider, for example, ten prisoners who are about to be executed for the same crime; it does not make any sense for any among them to be attached to some and angry at others; after all, every one of them is about to die. The only sensible approach is to be kind and patient with each other; it would be foolish to argue, making a distinction between "you" and "I." Similarly, since we all share the same lot in life—suffering, impermanence, and afflictive emotions—what is the point of making a big deal about oneself and considering others to be less worthy!

THE DISADVANTAGES OF
SELF-CHERISHING AND THE
ADVANTAGES OF OTHER-CHERISHING

Now let us reflect on the results of self-cherishing and other-cherishing. Shantideva succinctly addresses this:

> If you do not switch your concern
> From your own happiness to relieving others' pain,
> Not only will you not achieve Buddhahood,
> There will be no pleasures while in cyclic existence.

From the depths of your being you need to view self-centeredness as faulty. Up until now self-cherishing and its partner, ignorance, have dwelt in the center of your heart. Whether as a bug or as a god, self-cherishing has molded your outlook, with ignorance egging it on, so you have sought your own happiness as much as you could. But all those actions intended to bring you happiness have only created a mess.

Now it is time to view self-cherishing and the illusion of inherent existence as unhelpful, as disadvantageous, as defective. Leave self-cherishing behind and take up cherishing others. Leave ignorance behind and take up the wisdom that realizes selflessness.

As Shantideva says:

> What need is there to say more?
> Look at the difference between these two:
> Ordinary persons act for their own welfare,
> Whereas the Buddha acts for others' welfare.

By looking after others, the Buddha perfected his own mind and body, realizing both his own welfare and that of others, achieving everlasting bliss and the highest possible ability to help others. We, on the other hand, by self-cherishing and placing the phantom of inherent existence as the center of our perspective, have landed in a muddle.

Through Buddha's teaching we have come to know a little about what to adopt and what to discard in our outlook and behavior, to view self-centeredness as faulty and other-centeredness as advantageous. We need to identify our belief in inherent existence as a false and ruinous outlook that produces all suffering; so instead we must generate realization of selflessness, and then increase it to a limitless state. This might seem difficult to achieve, but with practice it will happen.

As I often admit, I have not fully achieved either the altruistic intention to become enlightened or the view of emptiness, but I have come to the point of seeing that there are no other choices. To the degree that I have come to some understanding of the lack of inherent existence, I have a sense that the appearance of people and things as if they exist from their own side is unreal, and based on this I experience all these as like illusions, having a conflict between how they appear and how they actually exist. Though this is not a full realization, it makes a difference with respect to counterproductive emotions. Although at the beginning I found altruism to be difficult, as I gradually became familiar with it, it looked more and more possible, so I became genuinely enthusiastic about practicing it. From practice, my life has become happier. That is one hundred percent for sure.

With experience, practices that were learned in earlier stages of the path but were not fully realized increase in force. For instance, faith in teachers of spiritual training (learned at the first level) increases by really seeing the value of what they teach and appreciating their kindness when you implement the teachings on emptiness (taught in the middle and high levels). With progress toward realizing emptiness, the act of seeking refuge in Buddha, his doctrine, and the spiritual community gains in strength, as does the intention not to waste the good fortune of this human life, as does contemplation of impermanence. Many earlier practices come into their own when later ones are experienced.

Indeed, there is a definite order with regard to developing an altruistic intention to become enlightened, since such altruism is based on having great compassion, which in turn must be preceded by developing an intention to become free from cylic existence. In these cases the earlier practices are foundations for the later ones, and without them the later ones cannot be generated in full. Nevertheless, relative to your background, level of intelligence, and interests, there are other types of practices for which the order may not be so strict. For instance, when you are contemplating unfavorable transmigration in cyclic existence and you consider how such a lifetime is driven by ignorance with respect to the effects of actions, this is part of the practices of a person of lesser capacity. But when you reflect on the fact that such a lifetime is also impelled by a deeper ignorance of the nature of all things, this is included within the practices of a person of middle capacity.

Therefore, when training in the stages of the path, it is important to identify the steps of meditative cultivation at each level and get some experience of them, but instead of waiting for each of those stages to dawn in full flowering, it is better to proceed with the higher levels, thereby mixing in their potency, much like taking a variety of mutually supportive medicines. This will likely be more effective.

Contemplation

1. Take this thought to heart:

   All sentient beings, through and through, are similar to me in wanting happiness and not wanting suffering. All of us want happiness and want to get rid of suffering. Therefore, how could it be right to have lust for some and hatred for others! I should help achieve happiness for all!

   Then consider this:

   All sentient beings exclusively want true happiness but do not possess it. No matter whom I might consider in the realms of cyclic existence, they are undergoing the suffering of pervasive conditioning. Given this, whom could I single out to consider close! Whom could I single out to consider distant!

2. Imagine ten beggars, all of whom are equally destitute, and consider how groundless it is to have good feelings for some and not for others.

3. Imagine ten sick persons who are equally ill; how could you be close to some and distant from others?

   ### How Everyone Has Helped You

4. Consider how everyone has helped you. All sentient beings have directly or indirectly provided services that have benefitted you; regardless of their motivation they have been kind to you.

5. All the comforts of this life are dependent upon other sentient beings. Reflect in detail on how your food, clothing,

residence, friendship, reputation, and possessions all come by way of other sentient beings.

6. Your present human life comes from moral actions in previous lives performed in relation to others.

7. Long life, freedom from illness, resources, creditable speech, and strength all come from moral actions in former lives.

8. Attainment of a good future life is based on moral actions performed in relation to sentient beings.

9. Morality is based on the principle that we must do no harm to others, thus other sentient beings are essential; without them you cannot perform virtuous deeds that keep them from harm. The virtue of refraining from killing requires other beings, as does refraining from stealing, sexual misconduct, and most other misdeeds. Without other sentient beings, these virtues could not be practiced.

10. Since morality is the very foundation of concentrated meditation and wisdom, even liberation from cyclic existence is due to sentient beings.

11. Attainment of Buddhahood relies on others, since the distinctive practices for achieving that state are love, compassion, and the altruistic intention to become enlightened, which come from taking notice of suffering beings and being moved from the depths of your heart to bring help and happiness to them. Hence we should respect them as much as we respect the Buddha.

12. Enemies are particularly valuable for cultivating love and compassion because anger destroys love and compassion, and the antidote to anger is patience, which can be practiced only toward someone harming you. Since enemies provide

a valuable opportunity for practicing such forbearance and tolerance, they are very valuable, even kind.

13. Unlike a doctor who brings pain in order to help, an enemy harms you intentionally; this is how an enemy provides a chance to cultivate patience.

THERE IS NO GOOD REASON FOR BEING EGOCENTRIC

14. A suitable reason for considering only yourself worthwhile and neglecting everyone else simply does not exist. For both you and others are equally stuck in cyclic existence with the burden of a mind-body system driven by afflictive emotions and karma.

15. Both you and others are facing imminent impermanence and death.

16. Imagine ten prisoners who are about to be executed for the same crime; it does not make sense for one among them to be attached to certain prisoners and to be angry at others. The only sensible course for them is to be kind and patient with one another; it would be foolish to argue, making a distinction between "you" and "I."

17. Similarly, all of us have fallen under the influence of suffering, impermanence, and afflictive emotions. Given that this is our situation, what is the point of making a big deal about yourself and considering others to be beneath you!

THE DISADVANTAGES OF SELF-CHERISHING AND THE ADVANTAGES OF OTHER-CHERISHING

18. Up till now, self-cherishing and its partner, ignorance, have taken up residence in the center of your heart. Despite drawing you into all sorts of actions to bring you happiness, these attitudes have only created a mess. You need

to view self-centeredness as faulty from the depths of your being.

19. Now it is time to leave self-cherishing behind and take up cherishing others, to leave ignorance behind and take up the wisdom that realizes selflessness.

20. By looking after others, the Buddha perfected his own mind and body, providing for both his own welfare and that of others, achieving perpetual bliss and the greatest possible ability to help others. We should do the same.

21. Though this might seem difficult to achieve, with time and effort it will happen.

That is the way to develop a sense of equality with others that motivates you to bring help and happiness to everyone everywhere.

17

Viewing Reality

All afflictive emotions are overcome
Through overcoming ignorance.

—ARYADEVA,

FOUR HUNDRED STANZAS

When listening to religious teachings, meditating, or the like it is important to establish your motivation beforehand. Our fundamental impetus should be to seek to quickly remove the three poisons of lust, hatred, and ignorance in all their gross and subtle forms—to refuse to voluntarily rush into them, to oppose them. This establishes as your motivation that you are heading toward liberation from cyclic existence.

In addition, you need to seek to engage in the behavior, the deeds, of Bodhisattvas. This establishes that you will not just seek to overcome the destructive emotions in your own continuum but will also strive to help all sentient beings overcome their afflictive emotions. Since to accomplish the final well-being of others it is necessary not only to defeat your counterproductive emotions but also to remove the predispositions they have left in your mind, you need to train in a complete path that is a means of purification, the practices of Bodhisattvas. Inspired by altruism rooted in love and compassion, you seek to practice the six perfections—giving, morality, patience, effort, concentration, and wisdom. In this chapter we will focus on the practice of the perfection of wisdom.

THE TWO MAIN SYSTEMS

There are two principal systems that Buddha used to teach the profound view of emptiness in accordance with the mental outlook of trainees. The chief expositors of these views were Nagarjuna and Asanga, whose lives had been prophesied by the Buddha. They are called "openers of chariot ways" because of their thorough descriptions of these views in accordance with the word of the Buddha.

In terms of the vast deeds of compassion, Nagarjuna and Asanga did not differ (though Asanga wrote more about this), but in terms of the profound view of emptiness they presented different perspectives. Nagarjuna's specific transmission was the view of the Middle Way School, and Asanga's was the view of the Mind-Only School. It seems to me that when an unbiased, discerning person investigates these two approaches, the view presented by Nagarjuna holds up completely. However, when we analyze the view of Mind-Only presented by Asanga, uncomfortable contradictions emerge.

According to the Mind-Only view, the mind itself is truly established. Indeed, the Mind-Only explanation that appearances of external objects are not truly established helps in diminishing our attachment to them. However, it is difficult to deemphasize the seeming solidity of mental experiences themselves. It is likely that our experiences of pleasure and pain would be taken to exist in the concrete way they appear to our consciousness.

According to Nagarjuna's Middle Way view, *all* phenomena, whether external or internal, are empty of inherent existence. Thus no matter what you are considering—objects of mind such as visible forms or your own mind—all of these are understood as not existing the way they appear to be. This is how Nagarjuna's deeper Middle Way view helps; it is very effective at counteracting our misconceptions and all the entanglements to which they lead.

THE ANTIDOTE TO IGNORANCE

Once our ignorant beliefs lead to suffering, if we want to get rid of our ignorance it will require more than mere wishing. To eliminate it, we must counter this misguided outlook. Whereas destructive emotions such as lust can be temporarily diminished in force through, for instance, imaginative meditation, to eradicate misconceptions about the nature of things we must generate wisdom that contradicts the misapprehensions of ignorance. To do this, you need to generate the particular discriminating insight that realizes the truth of selflessness. The source of the trouble is overcome through the wisdom that is its antidote.

THE PROCESS OF MISTAKE

Let us look into the process of misapprehension that is the root of cyclic existence. What is the deepest ignorance? It is the belief that things are as they appear, that they exist in their own right without depending on thought. Ignorance prevents us from seeing the truth, the fact that things are empty of the status they appear to have. This mistaken belief destroys our own well-being and that of others.

The misconception that the mind-body complex has its own inherent existence leads to mistakenly seeing "I" as inherently existent. This, in turn, leads to misguided actions that themselves make for more rebirths, more trouble. In this way, ignorance about mental and physical phenomena keeps us trapped in cyclic existence. As Nagarjuna's *Precious Garland of Advice* says:

> As long as the mind-body complex is misapprehended,
> So long thereby does the misapprehension of "I" exist.
> Further, when misapprehension of "I" exists,
> There is action, and from it there also is birth.

Misconstruing mental and physical phenomena as inherently existent precedes mistaking the self, or "I," as inherently existent, but both lie at the root of cyclic existence, since they both misconceive their respective objects the same way. Also, both bring on a host of desires and hatreds. When Chandrakirti, for instance, says that all afflictive emotions and defects arise from misapprehension of "I," he is referring to both of these misconceptions.

TWO TYPES OF SELFLESSNESS

Bear with me while I provide a little detail. In conceiving yourself to inherently exist, the "I" is being falsely seen as established from its own side. The time between the initial misapprehension of the mind-body complex and subsequent misapprehension of "I" is so brief, it seems as if the consciousness misconceiving the nature of "I" is also observing the mental and physical aggregates, but actually it is observing just "I."

Look at it this way: We are mainly concerned with

1. the person, or "I," who acts, accumulates karma, and as a result experiences pleasure and pain;
2. the phenomena that are experienced.

For this reason, in Buddhism there is a division of what exists into persons (including all types of living beings) and phenomena. Indeed persons are phenomena, but for the sake of understanding the importance of both the persons who are the experiencers and the phenomena that are experienced, there is a division into persons and (other) phenomena.

Once we put everything that exists into these two categories, we now have two types of ignorance—one that mistakenly perceives persons to inherently exist and another that misconceives other phenomena to inherently exist. Both are ignorance.

Whether you mistake yourself or another person as inherently existent, these are both misconceptions of persons. Mistaking the fundamental nature of your own or others' bodies, minds, eyes, ears, and so on as inherently existent is called a misconception of phenomena, as are misapprehensions of houses, trees, and so on.

Based on these same categories, there is an absence of inherent existence in persons, called a selflessness of persons, and an absence of inherent existence of other things called a selflessness of phenomena. As Chandrakirti says:

"Self" is a status of things that does not rely on others—inherent existence. Its nonexistence is selflessness. Through the division of phenomena and persons, selflessness is understood as twofold, "selflessness of persons and selflessness of (other) phenomena."

Between the two selflessnesses there is no difference in subtlety, since each is an emptiness of inherent existence.

The Need for Analysis

Do appearance and reality agree or disagree? Is there a conflict between how things seem and how they exist? Nowadays particle physicists describe a situation that is completely unlike the way things appear to us in ordinary perception. For example, a massive, ancient stone pillar seems hard and immovable; this is how it appears, but when we look closely at the particles that compose it, we see these particles rapidly change in each instant; its appearance and its being are not in accord. Within ordinary phenomena there are many such conflicts between appearance and reality.

In an even deeper way, when we are not satisfied with the way objects appear but look into their actual mode of being, we are finally left with nothing to point at that we can call the object. Due to this conflict between appearance and reality, Buddhist systems present a doctrine of two truths. The Middle Way School describes things that operate within the context of appearance to create help, harm, pleasure, pain, and so forth as "conventional truths," and then speaks of the reality beyond these appearances, which is discovered through analysis and is called "ultimate truth." Within one object there is an entity as it appears to conventional valid cognition, and an entity of deeper reality found by final analysis.

Persons and other phenomena do indeed exist; it is not that they do not exist. They help and harm. All of them are established through thoughts, but when we interact with them we feel that there is something over there in and of itself. For example, when we say, "Your chair is over there," and point at it, the chair seems to be something independent of being thought of; it seems to have all its capacities right in itself. However, if it actually were there in its own right as it appears to be, then as you analyzed it, it should become clearer and clearer, but it does not. When you search for things analytically, you cannot find them to exist in such a solid way. This indicates that there is a conflict between appearance and reality. Their concrete appearance is due to a fault of our minds.

This distortion occurs both in sense perception and in thought. Even in sense perception, phenomena appear in a false aspect due to faults embedded deep in our minds. And because of this false appearance, we are automatically drawn into believing that phenomena exist in their own right, much like assenting to false appearances in dreams. What is happening is that you are taking a basic, false appearance to be true, and then giving it many attributes through improper, counterproductive thinking. This generates a clutter of afflictive emotions.

Innate Ignorance

The *innate* form of ignorance—mistaking persons and other phenomena to exist in and of themselves—which all of us share, from insects on up, is the root cause of cyclic existence. It is not possible for a type of misconception that is merely *learned* from misguided systems to be the root of cyclic existence; such a root has to function with or without a mistaken system or inadequate reflection. For instance, the sophisticated but misguided notion, often found in non-Buddhist Indian systems, that a person has the three qualities of permanence, unity, and operating under her or his own power is only learned behavior—it is not innate: it only comes from contact with a system making an assertion based on misguided analysis.

Also, some systems assert that the minute particles making up physical objects have no parts. However, if that were the case, then a group of particles would not be any bigger than a single particle. The building blocks of physical objects must have parts since they must have dimension, no matter how small. Otherwise, how could one particle be next to another? How could a group of particles form a mass—like atoms forming a molecule?

Similarly, some systems put forward the notion that the single smallest moment of consciousness has no parts—no beginning, middle, or end. But again, if a moment of consciousness had no parts, then many moments together could not constitute a stream of consciousness; a continuum of mind could not form.

Such notions arise only in persons educated in a mistaken system: they do not arise in the uneducated. Therefore, this kind of artificially generated ignorance cannot serve as the root of cyclic existence that includes us all. Rather, the root problem must be a type of misunderstanding that has always existed in all beings, whether educated or uneducated. It must be innate, whereas the other types are artificial in the sense that they are learned. Innate ignorance here refers to becoming cognizant of any object, person, or other phenomenon, and accepting its appearance as existing on its own, truly existing, ultimately existing, existing without any conflict between how it appears and how it actually is.

The purpose of cultivating insight into reality through meditation is to attain liberation, and since innate ignorance is what binds beings in cyclic existence, the artificial forms of ignorance built on top of this basic ignorance are not the principal concern. What needs to be stopped are the innate ideas that lie at the root of all problems. When the innate is stopped, learned misconceptions are automatically eliminated. Still, getting rid of artificially generated mistakes helps toward that goal.

SEEING EVERYTHING AS LIKE AN ILLUSION

When through meditative analysis you realize the lack of inherent existence, or emptiness, within yourself, you understand for the first time that your self and other phenomena are false; they appear to exist in their own right but do not. You begin to see phenomena as being *like* illusions—recognizing the appearance of phenomena yet at the same time understanding that they are empty of existing the way they appear. Just as physicists distinguish between what appears and what actually exists, we need to recognize that there is a discrepancy between appearance and actual fact.

When encountering various good and bad objects, you should not be attached to their appearance but see them as being like illusions; this will keep you from coming under the influence of harmful emotions like lust or anger. If you see objects as existing inherently, obscuration sets in such that if the object is favorable, you become attached to it, thinking, "This is really wonderful." Once desire increases, anger will arise against whoever or whatever might interfere with your enjoyment. However, if you view the object as being like a magician's illusion that seems to exist inherently but does not, then instead of your perception of the object harming your life and practice, it helps. This is crucial because we have to make use of conventional outlooks within knowing the ultimate status of the phenomena with which we are dealing.

To see phenomena as being like illusions, it is necessary first to analyze whether phenomena really do exist the way they seem to exist. Analysis is not a matter of belief, and thus requires investigation from many angles. To do this, it is necessary to rely on wise people, but reliance does not mean just putting faith in them. Reliance means listening to them carefully and often, without being distracted by externals such as speaking or writing style, but applying the teachings internally to your own mental continuum.

You need to develop three levels of wisdom:

- first the "wisdom arisen from hearing," which means becoming capable of properly identifying the teachings either from listening to another's explanation or from reading;
- then the "wisdom arisen from thinking," which means to develop confidence from repeatedly engaging in analytical thinking, to the point where you do not waver if someone else says it is not so;
- and finally the "wisdom arisen from meditation," which arises from meditative familiarization repeated to the point of utter conviction.

Contemplation

1. All phenomena, whether external or internal, are empty of being truly established, empty of inherent existence.
2. No matter what you consider—visible forms, sounds, odors, tastes, and touches, or your own mind that is observing them—understand that these are empty of existing in and of themselves; they do not exist the way they appear.
3. To eradicate ignorance it is necessary to generate wisdom that contradicts it.
4. First the mind-body complex is misunderstood as existing inherently, and this leads to the misconception of "I" as be-

ing inherently existent. This, in turn, induces misguided actions that make for more rebirths, more suffering.

5. Based on the fact that we are mainly concerned with 1) the
person, or "I," who acts, accumulates karma, and as a result
experiences pleasure and pain and 2) the phenomena that
are experienced, we can distinguish two types of ignorance:
one that believes persons exist inherently and another that
sees all other phenomena as existing inherently.

6. In truth, persons exist but without inherent existence, and
this is called the selflessness of persons; when it comes to
other phenomena such as eyes, ears, body, mind, mountain,
and the like, this is called the selflessness of phenomena.
These two emptinesses are equally subtle.

7. It is necessary to differentiate between how phenomena appear to us and how they actually exist in fact.

8. Persons and other phenomena actually depend on thought,
but when we interact with them we feel that there is something over there in and of itself, independent of being thought
of, having all its capacities right in itself.

9. If it is actually there in its own right as it appears to be, then
as you analyze it, it should become clearer and clearer, but it
does not; you cannot find anything that exists in such a solid
way. When you delve deep enough into its being, you are finally left with nothing to point at that is the object.

10. Even in sense perception, phenomena falsely appear concrete
due to faults in our minds, and because of this false appearance, we are automatically drawn into conceiving that phenomena exist in their own right, much like assenting to false
appearances in dreams. An unfounded appearance is taken
to be true, and then we add many other attributes through

improper, counterproductive thinking, creating a mess of afflictive emotions.

11. Due to this conflict between appearance and reality, the Middle Way School speaks of entities that create help, harm, and so forth, calling them "conventional truths"; then it speaks of the reality beyond these appearances, which is called "ultimate truth." In one object, such as your body, its appearance can be found by conventional valid cognition, and its mode of being can be found by final analysis.

12. Innate ignorance takes cognizance of any object, a person or any other phenomenon, and assents to its appearance as inherently existent, existing by way of its own character, existing as its own reality, existing as its own mode of being, truly existing, ultimately existing, existing without any conflict between how it appears and how it actually is.

13. When through meditative analysis you realize the emptiness of inherent existence, you understand that you and all other phenomena seem to exist one way but actually do not. You see phenomena as being like illusions, with a discrepancy between their appearance and the actual truth of their existence.

14. Viewing persons and things as having this conflict between appearance and fact, like a magician's illusions, will keep you from coming under the influence of destructive emotions.

15. To see phenomena as being like illusions, it is necessary first to analyze whether phenomena really do exist the way they seem to exist.

18

The Way to Analyze

Those which arise dependently
Do not exist by way of their own nature.
—BUDDHA

This chapter encapsulates the methods of analysis in a series of contemplations that show how to perform analytical meditation on emptiness.

Contemplation

Consider:

1. We are at the center of all our troubles.
2. It is therefore best to work at understanding our true nature first.
3. After that this realization can be applied to the mind, the body, the house, the car, money, and all other phenomena.

FIRST STEP: GETTING A HOLD OF THE SELF YOU STRONGLY BELIEVE IN

1. Imagine that someone else criticizes you for something you actually did not do, saying, "You ruined such-and-such," and points a finger at you.

2. Watch your reaction. How does the "I" appear to your mind?

3. In what way are you apprehending it?

4. Notice how that "I" seems to stand by itself, self-instituting, established by way of its own character.

SECOND STEP: DETERMINING THE CHOICES

1. Analyze whether the "I" that is inherently self-established in the context of the mind-body complex could have a way of existing other than being part of the mind and body or separate from them.

2. Decide that if the "I" inherently exists as it seems to, then it must be either one with or separate from mind and body.

THIRD STEP: ANALYZING ONENESS

Consider the consequences if the "I" is established in and of itself, as it appears to our minds. If it is the *same* as mind-body:

1. "I" and mind-body would have to be utterly and absurdly in all ways one.

2. In that case, asserting the separate existence of an "I" absurdly would be pointless.

3. It absurdly would be impossible to think of "my body," or "my head," or "my mind."

4. When the body no longer exists, the self absurdly also would not exist.

5. Since mind and body are plural, one person's selves absurdly also would be plural.

6. Since the "I" is just one, mind and body absurdly also would be one.

7. Since mind and body are produced and disintegrate, it absurdly would have to be asserted that the "I" is inherently produced and inherently disintegrates, in which case either

the pleasurable effects of virtuous actions and the painful effects of nonvirtuous actions absurdly would not bear fruit for us, or absurdly we would be experiencing the effects of actions we ourselves did not commit.

Fourth Step: Analyzing Difference

Consider the consequences if the "I" is established in and of itself, as it appears to our minds, and if it is also inherently different from mind-body:

1. "I" and mind-body absurdly would have to be completely separate.
2. In that case, the "I" absurdly would have to be findable after clearing away the mind and body.
3. The "I" absurdly would not have the characteristics of being produced, abiding, and disintegrating.
4. Absurdly, the "I" would have to be either just a figment of the imagination or permanent.
5. Absurdly, the "I" would not have any physical or mental characteristics.

Coming to a Conclusion

1. If in the first step you got a fairly strong sense of how the "I" appears to be self-instituting and how you usually accept that appearance and then act on the basis of it, analysis will in time reveal that this sense of "I" is unfounded.
2. When that happens, remain in vivid awareness of the absence, the emptiness of such an inherently existent "I"; absorb the meaning of emptiness, and concentrate on the absence of inherent establishment.

Viewing Yourself as like an Illusion

1. Then, once again let your appearance and that of others dawn to your mind.

2. Remember a time when you mistook a reflection of a person in a mirror to be an actual person; it appeared to be a person but was not.

3. Similarly, all people and things seem to exist without depending on causes and conditions, on their parts, and on thought, but they do not. In this way, people and things are like illusions.

4. Reflect on the fact that within the context of dependent-arising you engage in actions and thus accumulate karma and experience the effects of those actions.

5. Consider the fact that the appearance of people is feasible within the absence of inherent existence.

6. When being viable and emptiness seem to be contradictory, use the example of a mirror image:

> The image of a face is undeniably produced in dependence on a face and a mirror, even though it is empty of the eyes, ears, and so forth it appears to possess, and the image of a face undeniably disappears when either face or mirror is absent. Similarly, even though a person does not have even a speck of inherent establishment, it is not contradictory for a person to perform actions, accumulate karma, experience effects, and to be born in dependence on karma and destructive emotions.

7. Try to see the lack of contradiction between being viable and emptiness with respect to all people and things.

ALTERNATING ANALYTICAL AND
STABILIZING MEDITATION

Remember that when you are analyzing, you need mindfulness to stay focused on the object and investigate its nature, in order to keep from straying to other objects. Also, during your analytical search you need to make use of introspection to determine whether you are about to become distracted. If so, you should switch to stabilizing meditation, concentrating just on the meaning found through analysis. This will bring your concentration back full force.

The goal is to get to a solid footing, where analytical meditation itself brings about a stable undistracted mind as well as mental and physical flexibility. By repeatedly moving back and forth between 1) stabilizing meditation in which you just focus on a single object and 2) analytical meditation, you will get to a point where these two modes of meditation will eventually promote each other. Then, operating within stabilization itself, you will be capable of strong analysis, which itself will bring about even greater stability.

19

Buddhahood

Just as you are intent on thinking
Of what could be done to help yourself,
So you should be intent on thinking
Of what could be done to help others.

—Nagarjuna,

Precious Garland

of Advice

Long ago, there must have been humans who, upon considering the situation of the world over the course of time, lost hope in
what they could accomplish by means of their own abilities; their
will was broken by discouragement. At that point they came to believe in what could not be seen with the eyes, and put their hope
in something beyond the range of normal vision. This must have
been how the initial development of religious groups occurred.

At the appropriate moment in the progress of human thought,
Buddha appeared in India after training for many lives in the altruistic practices of Bodhisattvas. According to the biography of
Shakyamuni Buddha as it is known throughout the world, he was
born as a prince in a royal family and, despite being protected from
seeing the sufferings of the world, came in the course of his life to

see the ravages of old age, sickness, and death. These drove him to investigate whether there was a technique for being liberated from such sufferings, and if there was, how it could be implemented. At age twenty-nine he escaped from the palace, relinquishing the princely robes of his royal line, left the householder life, cut his hair, practiced asceticism for six years to achieve concentrated meditation, and ultimately became enlightened under the Bodhi tree at Bodh Gaya.

For forty-nine days Buddha did not immediately speak about what he had realized but considered who might be suitable to hear about it, and finally decided to teach five disciples the four noble truths. Then, after forty-five years of teaching, he displayed the signs of passing away into nirvana at age eighty-one.

His teaching stemming from the four noble truths occurred at a crucial juncture in human history; his ideas were so appropriate and meaningful that an exceptional religion based on the four truths sprang up and flourishes to this day. People the world over, regardless of whether they are Buddhist or not, are aware that there was someone called Gautama Buddha, praised for his profound and unique presentation on the nature of persons and objects and for his related teaching of the altruistic intention to become enlightened, in which others are cherished more than oneself.

Texts of his system that emphasize love, compassion, and the altruistic intention to become enlightened (called the Great Vehicle) speak of the Buddha as having practiced life after life over three periods of countless great eons to complete the requisite stores of merit and wisdom, and bring his development to perfection. If the effect of this altruistic training for such a hugely long period of time was merely teaching for forty-five years, as the usual history of Buddha presents it, this effect would be disproportionate to the cause of enlightenment, which requires great compassion to help countless beings. Also, if at the end of his life Buddha passed away in such a way that his consciousness was obliterated, as some claim, that would be incommensurate with the doctrine that full enlightenment has the feature of accomplishing others' welfare spontaneously, without exertion, for as long as space exists.

Indeed, when we consider whether the continuum of consciousness, which has a nature of luminosity and cognition, could ever be broken, we can determine that this would be impossible. If a luminous and cognitive mind were produced from a mistaken mind, then when the mistake was gradually removed, the luminous and cognitive mind would also gradually have to stop, but luminous cognition and misapprehension are entirely different. When wisdom undermines ignorance, this does not oppose the continuation of basic mind. It contradicts reason for an enlightened mind to be snuffed out.

SIMULTANEOUSLY REALIZING ALL

Enlightenment is a state of freedom not only from the counterproductive emotions that drive the process of cyclic existence but also from the predispositions established in the mind by those afflictive emotions. These subtle predispositions, or latent forces within the mind, see to it that whenever conventional phenomena come to your mind, the ultimate truth is not manifest, and when the ultimate truth is manifest to your mind, conventional phenomena cannot appear. This means that even when you arrive at the profound point of being able to directly realize the truth, during that deep realization other phenomena cannot appear to your mind, and later, when a conventional phenomenon appears to your mind, you cannot realize emptiness directly. Rather you must alternate between these two types of realizations—the wisdom that directly knows the truth, and the perception of ordinary phenomena.

In Buddhist terms this necessity of alternation is called the "defilement of apprehending the two truths as if they were different entities." When this defilement is extinguished, a single consciousness can take conventional phenomena to mind even while directly realizing the ultimate truth. It is then possible to simultaneously know everything, both the diversity of phenomena and their profound mode of being, emptiness. This is omniscience.

When you overcome not only the afflictive emotions preventing liberation from cyclic existence but also these more subtle defilements, at that point you have achieved a Buddha's "great enlightenment," a thorough purification of the sources of all problems and full comprehension of all that can be known.

THE POWER OF ENLIGHTENMENT

Great Vehicle scriptures tell us that when defilements associated with the mind are purified, you bring to fulfillment your capacities to effect both your own development and that of other beings. Since you have removed the limitation forcing you to alternate between direct realization of the profound reality of emptiness and paying attention to other phenomena, you have overcome all problems and have achieved realization of all knowables; now you can spontaneously bring about the well-being of others. Over countless eons you have practiced solely for the sake of others, so now your activities to help others come without exertion.

From beginningless time your mind has been empty of inherent existence, and now that your mind is also purified of all defilements, your emptiness of mind is called a Buddha's nature body. Your mind, which formerly merely contained the *seeds* of the qualities of Buddhahood, is now a Buddha's wisdom body.

For countless great eons you have single-mindedly practiced to benefit others with the altruistic attitude depicted in the prayerwish:

> May I at all times
> Be available for others' sake
> Just as earth, water, fire, wind, medicine,
> And forests should be available to all.

The result of this powerful development of altruistic will is that the capacities intrinsic to your mind have matured so that your mind and body are one undifferentiable entity. Even in ordinary life, the very subtle mind and energy that carries the very subtle mind are one entity, and now in the pure state of having completed the path, this basic fact of the undifferentiable entity of subtle mind and its energy allows you to manifest in manifold ways most appropriate to helping others. Among the forms you can take is a "complete enjoyment body," which, in accordance with earlier prayer-wishes, remains as long as space exists to relieve suffering with continuous altruistic activities for high-level practitioners. This complete enjoyment body also appears at appropriate moments in history as a "supreme emanation body" to teach the path to enlightenment. Shakyamuni Buddha was just such a being.

In Tibet, China, Japan, Korea, Mongolia, Taiwan, and Vietnam, those following the Great Vehicle and in particular the mode of instruction at Nalanda, India's prime center of Buddhist learning, speak of a Buddha as having four bodies—a nature body, a wisdom body, a complete enjoyment body, and an emanation body—or three bodies when the first two are treated as one, called "the body of attributes." In these countries, we say that our teacher Shakyamuni Buddha, who appeared in India more than 2,500 years ago, had become enlightened a long time earlier and appeared as a supreme emanation body in this world in India while at the same time appearing as appropriate in myriad other worlds in accordance with the dispositions and interests of sentient beings when the time is ripe.

These appearances can take various forms, including even a bridge or a ship as needed, or as a leader of a religion other than Buddhism, teaching attitudes such as love, compassion, tolerance, and contentment. Thus from a Buddhist's perspective many teachers of other religions could have been emanations of a Buddha or of a Bodhisattva. If Buddhas can appear even as a bridge or a ship, they could definitely appear as religious figures providing helpful teachings for millions of beings. Thus, from this standpoint as well as from seeing that the world's many religions are helpful for different types of persons, we should respect all religions as beneficial to society.

Contemplation

Consider:

1. It is impossible for the continuum of consciousness, which has a nature of luminosity and cognition, to ever be severed. When wisdom undermines ignorance, there is no condition that could oppose the continuation of basic mind.

2. Enlightenment is a state of freedom not only from the counterproductive emotions driving cyclic existence but also from

the predispositions established in the mind by those afflictive emotions.

3. These subtle predispositions are latent forces within the mind that see to it that, prior to Buddhahood, whenever conventional phenomena come to mind, the ultimate truth is not manifest, and whenever the ultimate truth is manifest to your mind, conventional phenomena cannot appear.

4. This necessity of alternation is called the "defilement of apprehending the two truths as if they were different entities." Due to this limitation you are forced to switch between direct realization of the profound reality and paying attention to everyday phenomena, but when this defilement is extinguished, a single consciousness can take conventional phenomena to mind even while it is also directly realizing the ultimate truth.

5. It is then possible to simultaneously know everything, both the diversity of phenomena and their profound mode of being, emptiness. This is omniscience, a Buddha's "great enlightenment," which is purification from the sources of all problems and full comprehension of all that can be known.

6. This state fulfills your capacity to effect both your own development and that of others. You have overcome all problems and have achieved realization of all knowables, which means that you can bring about the well-being of others spontaneously.

7. At Buddhahood you attain the four Buddha bodies:
   - Your mind has from beginningless time been empty of inherent existence, and now that your mind is purified of all defilements, the same emptiness is called a Buddha's *nature body*.

- Your mind, which formerly merely contained the *seeds* of the qualities of Buddhahood, is now a Buddha's *wisdom body.*

- Even in ordinary life, very subtle mind and the energy that drives very subtle mind are one entity, and now in the pure state of having completed the path, this basic fact allows you to manifest in countless ways in forms appropriate to helping others. Among these forms is a *complete enjoyment body*, which, in accordance with earlier prayer-wishes, remains as long as space exists to relieve suffering through continuous altruistic activities for high-level practitioners.

- The complete enjoyment body, in turn, appears in myriad worlds in various *emanation bodies* in accordance with the dispositions and interests of sentient beings when the time is ripe; it also appears at appropriate moments throughout history as a "supreme emanation body," to teach the path to enlightenment (Shakyamuni Buddha was such a being).

20

Reviewing the Steps

H ere is the entire set of contemplations for easily accessible cultivation of the path to enlightenment.

INITIAL LEVEL OF PRACTICE

Recognizing Our Fortunate Situation

Consider:

1. Presently you have a very fortunate situation, for you are free from obstacles to religious practice, and you possess many favorable attributes that enable you to achieve high spiritual development.

2. This situation is rare.

3. Attaining such a situation in the next lifetime requires fundamentally moral behavior, practicing generosity and so forth, and aiming their effects toward being reborn in a well-endowed human lifetime.

4. The bad effects of a nonvirtuous action can be mitigated in four ways: by disclosing it, by regretting having done it, by intending not to do it in the future, and by engaging in virtuous actions such as public service.

5. Virtuous deeds should be performed by preparing a good motivation in advance, with high-quality execution, and by dedicating its force to altruistic enlightenment at its conclusion, without regrets.

6. It is important to develop a distaste for destructive emotions.

7. Think to yourself:

> *Day and night I will make good use of this body of mine, which is a home of illness and the basis for the sufferings of old age, and lacks a core like a bubble.*

Knowing You Will Die

Consider:

1. The illusion of permanence, or being unaware of death, creates the counterproductive idea that you will be around for a long time; this, in turn, leads to superficial activities that undermine both yourself and others.

2. Awareness of death draws you into thinking about whether there is a future life and taking interest in the quality of that life, which promotes helpful long-term activities and diminishes dedication to the merely superficial.

3. To appreciate the imminence of death, think deeply about the implications of the three roots, nine reasons, and three decisions:

First root: Contemplation that death is definite

1. because death cannot be avoided
2. because our lifespan cannot be extended and grows ever shorter
3. because even when we are alive there is little time to practice.

FIRST DECISION: I MUST PRACTICE.

Second root: Contemplation that the time of death is uncertain

4. because our life span in this world is indefinite

5. because the causes of death are many and the causes of life are few

6. because the time of death is unknowable due to the fragility of the body.

SECOND DECISION: I MUST PRACTICE NOW.

Third root: Contemplation that at the time of death nothing helps except transformative practice

7. because at the time of death our friends are no help

8. because at the time of death our wealth is no help

9. because at the time of death our body is no help.

THIRD DECISION: I WILL PRACTICE NONATTACHMENT TO ALL OF THE WONDERFUL THINGS OF THIS LIFE.

4. Make sure not to develop strong lust or hatred near your time of death, since this could adversely influence your rebirth.

5. If you have engaged in many nonvirtues during your life, it is important near the end to develop strong contrition for what you have done; this will help your next life.

Thinking About Future Lives

Consider:

1. Material things such as your body depend upon various causes and conditions, which means there has to be a continuum of causes for such an entity. The material body stems from material provided by the parents, sperm and egg, which themselves stem from material provided by their parents, and so on.

2. Similarly, your consciousness depends upon its own causes and conditions, which points to a continuum of causes for the luminous and cognitive nature of your mind, which comes from former lives.

3. Also, given the vast range of differences between children of the same parents, it seems likely that cognitive predispositions from earlier lives are at work in this life.

4. Valid memory of previous lives confirms the existence of former lives. One person's valid memory indicates that such lives were experienced by all of us, whether or not we ourselves remember them.

5. There can be no beginning to the round of rebirth.

6. Just as a house is constructed by the builder, so the entire world that is our environment takes shape due to the karmic influences of the beings who live in the world, and from their past lifetimes over a long course of time.

7. Your own actions determine how you will be reborn, just as the world itself is shaped by the karmas of the beings who will inhabit it.

8. Reflect on the cause-and-effect relationship between actions and their fruits, understanding the implications.

9. Bring to mind the suffering of beings in a dire situation, including animals, and imagine yourself in a similarly exposed situation. This will inspire restraint from actions (karmas) producing a negative rebirth.

10. Work at avoiding the ten nonvirtues:
    • the three principal physical nonvirtues—killing, stealing, and sexual misconduct;
    • the four principal verbal nonvirtues—lying, divisive talk, harsh speech, and senseless chatter;

- the three principal mental nonvirtues—covetousness, harmful intent, and wrong views.

Identifying the Refuge

Consider these insights:

1. Mistaking people and things as having inherent existence gives rise to more mistaken thinking.

2. Mistaken thinking generates the afflictive emotions of lust, hatred, enmity, jealousy, belligerence, and laziness.

3. These destructive emotions lead to actions (karmas) that have been infected by these emotions.

4. These actions leave imprints in the mind that drive the painful round of repeated births.

5. Therefore, ignorance is the root of cyclic existence. Ignorance here means not just an absence of knowledge about how phenomena actually exist but an active misconception of the status of persons and things: seeing them as fully autonomous, or independent, entities.

6. This ignorance is uprooted by the realization that all phenomena are interrelated and interdependent entities.

7. If phenomena did indeed exist the way they appear to, that is, established on their own side, then by definition their dependence on other factors could not be possible, but your own experience shows you that interdependence is truly the way of things.

8. Through this route you can see that your own mental outlook mistakenly ascribes an exaggerated status to people and things; they do not exist in this way.

9. When you begin to see that this extreme assignment of virtue or evil to a person is what makes them an object of

lust or hatred, the emotion that is built on that exaggeration backs off; we see the mistake we have made, and we pull back.

10. Good and bad, favorable and unfavorable do exist, but not in the concrete way that they seem to when viewed by a lustful or a hateful mind.

11. Once you understand that lust and hatred are mistakes and that their root, the ignorant conception that phenomena exist in their own right, is also mistaken, you will know that the wisdom that realizes dependent-arising and emptiness is founded in valid cognition.

12. When you cultivate this insight more and more, it will become stronger and stronger because it is valid, and you will see that enlightenment is possible.

13. You will see in your experience that reflecting on dependent-arising and emptiness engenders insight that is helpful in daily life, which can develop into an incontrovertible understanding of emptiness and even direct perception of it. Even with a limited level of *valid experience* you can determine that there are *valid gurus* who can offer *valid commentaries* on Buddha's teachings, the *valid scriptures*. Based on these four validities, you can gain conviction in Buddhahood as profound and vast, as mentally and physically perfect.

14. By reflecting on the truth of dependent-arising and emptiness, you come to realize that it is possible to stop destructive thoughts through spiritual realizations in keeping with the Buddhist doctrine. Those who have some experience of these cessations and paths in their mental continua make up the spiritual community, and those who have brought this process of spiritual development to perfection are known as

Buddhas. When these appear to your mind, you will see the reasonableness of turning to the Buddha, his doctrine, and the spiritual community for refuge.

15. Taking your own situation as an example, you contemplate the fact that although all sentient beings throughout space want happiness and do not want suffering, they have come under the influence of suffering; seeking your own full enlightenment as an omniscient Buddha in order to help them, you turn to the Three Jewels for refuge. The realized doctrine is the actual refuge, the Buddha is the teacher of refuge, and the spiritual community includes those who help you attain that refuge.

Karma

Consider:

1. All pleasures, small or great, arise from virtuous actions, and all pains, great or small, arise from nonvirtuous actions.

2. Even small actions can have huge effects.

3. The three principal physical nonvirtues are killing, stealing, and sexual misconduct; the four principal verbal nonvirtues are lying, divisive talk, harsh speech, and senseless chatter; the three principal mental nonvirtues are covetousness, harmful intent, and wrong views.

4. Killing is weightier than stealing, which is weightier than sexual misconduct. Lying is weightier than divisive talk, which is weightier than harsh speech, which is weightier than senseless chatter. Wrong views are weightier than harmful intent, which is weightier than covetousness. The same order of weightiness holds also for the opposite virtues: refraining from killing and so forth.

5. Many factors influence the weight of virtuous and nonvirtuous actions: the intensity of motivation, habituation, whether
the action harms or helps beneficial people or groups, and
keenness for the action throughout life.

6. Actions become weightier depending on how they are undertaken.

7. The effects of actions can take four aspects: fruitional, impelling an entire new life; experiential, or similar to the cause
in experience; functional, or similar to the cause in a practical
way; environmental, or similar to the cause in terms of external surroundings.

8. Although a happy transmigration as a human or god is a fruitional effect of a virtuous karma, and a bad transmigration as
an animal, hungry ghost, or hell-being is a fruitional effect
of a nonvirtuous karma, the karmas that fill out the details
of that particular life situation still can be either virtuous or
nonvirtuous.

9. Among karmas, the weightiest ripen first, then karmas
aroused at death, then the habituated karmas, followed by
those that formed earliest.

10. Nonvirtuous karmas can begin ripening in the present lifetime if based on actions performed with excessive attachment to your body, resources, and life, or with strong malice
toward others, or with enmity toward those who have helped
you, or with great animosity toward sources of refuge such as
Buddha, the doctrine, and the spiritual community. Virtuous actions can begin ripening in the present lifetime if they
were undertaken without being overly concerned with your
own body, resources, and life, or if they were performed with
deep compassion and helpfulness, or with a strong attitude

of wishing to reciprocate for help given to you, or with deep faith and conviction. Otherwise, the effects will be experienced in the next lifetime or later lifetimes.

11. The force of virtuous deeds can be weakened by anger.

12. The capacity of a nonvirtuous karma to produce its effect will remain unless it is counteracted by the four forces: contrition, engaging in virtuous activities specifically for the sake of counteracting the impact of the nonvirtuous act, intending not to engage in it in the future, and building a foundation in refuge and the altruistic intention to become enlightened.

MIDDLE LEVEL OF PRACTICE

Seeing the Problem and the Cure

Consider:

1. Mind and body fall under the influence of destructive emotions, and the actions (karmas) driven by these counterproductive attitudes bind beings in temporary states as gods, demigods, humans, animals, hungry ghosts, and hell-beings.

2. The way out of this situation is to address afflictive emotions directly, which keeps previously accumulated karmas from being activated so they cannot manifest as a new lifetime of suffering. The karmas remaining in your mental continuum are thereby deactivated.

3. Liberation is a state of separation from the burden of living with a mind and body under the control of destructive emotions and karma.

4. There are four noble truths:

- External and internal phenomena that are fashioned from destructive emotions and karma are true sufferings.
- Afflictive emotions and karmas are the true origins of suffering.
- Pacification of afflictive emotions is liberation, or true cessation.
- The means for overcoming and pacifying afflictive emotions are known as true paths.

5. The first two of the four truths, suffering and its sources, indicate what we need to discard; the last two, cessations and paths, point out what we need to adopt.

6. Since all of us want happiness and do not want suffering, we must *recognize* the full extent of suffering, for then we will seek liberation from it. Once we decide we do not want these painful effects, we must *abandon* the destructive emotions that cause them, the sources of suffering. In order to achieve a cure we need to *actualize* the cessation of the sources of pain. To do this, we must *cultivate* the path.

7. If you do not have a strong intention to escape the clutches of pervasive conditioning by looking at its pernicious works, the development of thoroughgoing compassion will lie beyond your reach.

8. Counterproductive emotions are unpeaceful, uncomfortable, stressful, and disturbing.

9. Lust leads to anger when it is thwarted.

10. We bring trouble upon ourselves by mistaking the true nature of people, but also mistaking what is impure for pure, what is a state of pain for pleasure, and what is impermanent for permanent.

11. Our birth from afflictive emotions and karma means that we are prone to those same emotions, generating lust for the attractive, hatred for the unattractive, and confusion for what is neither.

12. If aging happened all at once, it would be intolerable.

13. Sickness puts the elements of the body out of balance, bringing physical pain that in turn promotes mental pain, which weakens vitality and makes fulfillment impossible.

14. We suffer from seeing that death will separate us from nice objects, nice relatives, and nice friends, and while dying we may undergo many discomforts.

15. Our mind-body complex serves as a basis for present suffering (projected by earlier afflictive emotions and karmas) that plays itself out in aging, sickness, and death, and our usual responses to painful situations promotes future suffering.

16. By being associated with dysfunctional tendencies, our mind-body complex induces outright suffering; the very existence of this sort of mind and body is itself an expression of the suffering of pervasive conditioning.

17. Since pain and pleasure arise from causes and conditions, these feelings are subject to techniques that bring relief.

18. Between the two origins of suffering—contaminated actions and afflictive emotions—afflictive emotions (lust, hatred, and ignorance) are the primary cause, and among those counterproductive emotions ignorance is chief, because lust and hatred arise from exaggeration of the status of an object beyond what actually exists.

19. When you see that this ignorance can be eliminated because it lacks the support of valid cognition, you become deter-

mined to tame your mind to achieve what is known as cessation.

20. The presence of opposing forces indicates the potential for change; when you need to counteract something, first you identify its opposing force, and when you increase its power, the strength of its opposite diminishes. Since suffering is caused by afflictive emotions, relying on attitudes that oppose them promotes healthy change.

21. Chief among the paths leading to freedom is direct realization of selflessness (the emptiness of inherent existence) because this has the power to serve as an actual antidote to the source of suffering. This special training in wisdom requires concentrated meditation, which in turn depends on training in morality. Thus the amelioration of suffering relies on three trainings—morality, concentrated meditation, and wisdom.

The Implications of Impermanence

Consider:

1. Things made by causes change moment by moment.

2. The causes of a phenomenon themselves make it have a nature of disintegration from the start.

3. Impermanent phenomena are totally under the influence of the causes and conditions that produce them.

4. Our present mind-body complex does not operate under its own power but under the influence of past causes, specifically ignorance. This indicates that it is under the sway of suffering.

5. That our mind-body complex appears to exist under its own power but does not underscores the conflict between its appearance and reality.

6. Wisdom calls for perceiving phenomena to be empty of the way they seem to exist; this is how it can oppose the mistakes made through the ignorant view that phenomena exist independently.

7. Thorough development of wisdom yields the peace of passing beyond suffering, yields nirvana.

HIGH LEVEL OF PRACTICE

Altruism

Consider:

1. We like life stories motivated by altruism, whereas hearing about the lives of those whose actions stemmed from wanting to harm others evokes fear and apprehension.

2. A beautiful internal attitude is more important than external beauty.

3. Only you can make your mind beautiful.

4. Working at achieving the welfare of others accomplishes your own along the way.

5. What needs to be stopped is not concern for your own development but self-cherishing in which almost the entire focus of attention is on yourself.

6. Lust fails to draw together what is favorable to ourselves because at its core it is biased and therefore stupid. In lust what seems to be affection for another is prejudiced, which allows hatred to set in upon even slight interference.

7. Altruism is supremely effective at drawing beneficial factors together because it is in accord with the very nature of interdependence, which lies at the heart of social interaction.

8. True happiness and freedom from suffering can be realized only from a broad outlook; it cannot be seen from a narrow perspective.

9. With lust and hatred, your outlook is necessarily constricted. By focusing on just one particular factor among the many giving rise to a problem, you close the door to broadmindedness.

10. Afflictive emotions require a seemingly real and autonomous target.

11. The broader your outlook is, the greater the possibility of constructing something positive or undoing something negative.

12. Focusing only on yourself is the problem; being concerned for others is the solution.

13. Understanding interdependence is relevant in myriad fields because it provides a holistic outlook. Altruism is the door for opening up this broad view.

14. When you are solely concerned with "I," this naturally leads to fear and anxiety, resulting in even more insecurity, making even the body imbalanced.

15. The world can be transformed as each of us changes our attitude; this change will spread from person to person.

16. The way to rise to a higher level of spiritual practice is to develop altruism to the point where seeking enlightenment in order to serve others more effectively becomes your inner, spontaneous motivation for everything you do.

Engendering Great Compassion

FOUNDATIONAL STEP: FREEING YOUR RELATIONSHIPS FROM BIAS

1. Imagine a friend, an enemy, and a neutral person standing before you.
2. With one part of your mind consider your attitudes toward your enemy, your friend, and the neutral person.
3. Does your enemy appear to be completely unattractive, having harmed you or your friends in this life?
4. Does your friend appear to be completely attractive, having helped you or your intimates in this life?
5. Does the neutral person appear to be neither of these?
6. Consider that over the course of many lifetimes and even within this present lifetime there is no certainty at all that an enemy will remain an enemy, a friend will remain a friend, or that a neutral person will remain neutral.
7. Decide therefore that it is not right to single out just one group for intimacy, another just for indifference, and yet another solely for alienation.
8. Consider that all beings are the same; they want happiness and not suffering, just as you do. Reflecting this way will remove bias.

FIRST STEP: FINDING EVERYONE DEAR

Consider:

1. Once it becomes clear that consciousness has to be produced from a cause of similar type, the continuum of your mind has to be beginningless.
2. Once you see that the continuum of your mind has no beginning, the person that is founded in dependence upon that continuum of consciousness also could have no beginning.

3. Once the person, or "I," has no beginning, you must have taken rebirth over and over.

4. Hence there is no saying that in the cyclic existence of birth and death you did not take rebirth in any particular place or with any particular type of body.

5. The bodies assumed in those births must have been of various types, including birth from a womb (human and animal) and birth from an egg (birds and so forth).

6. Most births from a womb or from an egg require a nurturer, someone to look after you.

7. There is no saying that any particular being has not taken care of you and will not do so again in the future.

8. In this fundamental sense everyone is close to you, intimate.

SECOND STEP: BEING AWARE OF HOW EVERYONE HELPED

1. Call to mind the many ways, whether animal or human, that a mother or other caregiver nurtures the child.

2. Consider how, whether born as an animal or a human, a child puts hope in and generates affection for the nurturer.

3. Reflect on this situation until feeling stirs in you.

4. Realize that at some time over the course of countless lifetimes your friends have nurtured you in this way, and acknowledge their kindness.

5. Realize that at some time over the course of lifetimes neutral persons have nurtured you in this way, and acknowledge their kindness.

6. Realize that at some time over the course of lifetimes your enemies have nurtured you in this way, and acknowledge their kindness.

In this way you will gradually become mindful of the intimate kindnesses that all beings have extended to you.

THIRD STEP: RECIPROCATING OTHERS' KINDNESS

Consider:

1. All the motherly sentient beings who have kindly provided for you over the course of lifetimes undergo physical and mental pain.

2. Also, they are weighed down by having performed deeds that will create future suffering.

3. In addition, they are presently headed in the direction of actions that will result in more pain.

4. It would be vulgar not to return their kindness.

5. The best reciprocation would be to help them achieve the stable, lasting peace and bliss of liberation from cyclic existence and the full physical and mental perfection of Buddhahood.

6. Imagine:

   Your mother is crazed, blind, guideless, stumbling with every step as she nears a cliff. If she cannot place hope in her child for help, in whom can she put trust? If her child does not take responsibility for freeing her from this terror, who would take responsibility? Her child must set her free. In the same way, the madness of afflictive emotions disturbs the peace of mind of living beings, your nurturers. Having no control over their minds, they are crazed; they lack eyes to see the way to a favorable rebirth and to the definite goodness of liberation and omniscience. They have no true teacher, a guide for the blind. They stumble from their wrongdoing, crippling them at each moment. When these motherly beings see the edge of the precipice of cyclic existence in general and the miserable realms in particular, they naturally put hope in their children, and their children naturally have a responsibility to get their mothers out of this situation.

With this in mind, train in the intention to reciprocate the kindness of your infinite mothers by helping them achieve release from suffering and limitation.

FOURTH STEP: CULTIVATING LOVE

1. Imagine your best friend in front of you and meditate on each of the three strengths of love until you deeply feel it:
   — This person wants happiness but is deprived. *How nice it would be* if she or he could be imbued with happiness and all of its causes!
   — This person wants happiness but is deprived. *May* she or he be imbued with happiness and all its causes.
   — This person wants happiness but is deprived. *I will do whatever I can* to help her or him to be imbued with happiness and all the causes of happiness!
2. Extend this meditation to more friends, one by one.
3. Imagine a neutral person in front of you and meditate on each of the three strengths of love until you deeply feel it:
   — This person wants happiness but is deprived. *How nice it would be* if she or he could be imbued with happiness and all of its causes!
   — This person wants happiness but is deprived. *May* she or he be imbued with happiness and all its causes.

— This person wants happiness but is deprived. *I will do what-ever I can* to help her or him to be imbued with happiness and all the causes of happiness!

4. Extend this meditation to more neutral persons, one by one.

5. Imagine your least enemy in front of you and meditate on each of the three strengths of love until you deeply feel it:

— This person wants happiness but is deprived. *How nice it would be* if she or he could be imbued with happiness and all of its causes!

— This person wants happiness but is deprived. *May she or he be imbued with happiness and all its causes.*

— This person wants happiness but is deprived. *I will do what-ever I can* to help her or him to be imbued with happiness and all the causes of happiness!

6. Extend this meditation to more enemies, one by one.

Also, when watching the news or reading the newspaper about beings in awful situations such as famine, flood, and extreme pov-erty, consider:

1. These beings are all like myself in wanting happiness and in having the right to gain happiness, but due to external and internal circumstances they find themselves in dire straits.

2. Think, "What an awful situation! May they have happiness!"

FIFTH STEP: COMPASSION

As with love, compassion is to be cultivated first toward your friends, then neutral beings, and finally enemies. Meditate on each of the three increasing strengths of compassion until you deeply feel it.

1. Imagine your best friend in front of you and meditate on each of the three levels of compassion as follows:
   — This person wants happiness and not suffering, yet is stricken with outright physical and mental pain, the pain of change, and the pain of pervasive conditioning. *How nice it would be* if he or she could only be free from suffering and the causes of suffering!
   — This person wants happiness and not suffering, yet is stricken with outright physical and mental pain, the pain of change, and the pain of pervasive conditioning. *May he or she be free* from suffering and the causes of suffering!
   — This person wants happiness and not suffering, yet is stricken with outright physical and mental pain, the pain of change, and the pain of pervasive conditioning. *I will do whatever I can* to help him or her be free from suffering and the causes of suffering!
2. Extend this meditation to more friends, one by one.
3. Imagine a neutral person in front of you and meditate on each of the three strengths of compassion until you feel it deeply.
4. Extend this meditation to more neutral persons, one by one.
5. Imagine your least enemy in front of you and meditate on each of the three strengths of compassion until you deeply feel it.
6. Extend this meditation to more enemies, one by one.

SIXTH STEP: TOTAL COMMITMENT

To develop this supreme altruistic will:
1. Take to mind again and again the meaning of this stanza from Shantideva's *A Guide to the Bodhisattva's Way of Life:*

As long as space remains and there are
transmigrating beings,
May I remain relieving the sufferings of sentient
beings.

2. Remember to dedicate all your virtuous activities and the beneficial karmas established in your mind stream to the benefit of all sentient beings.

3. Resolve:

Even if I have to do it alone, I will free all sentient beings from suffering and the causes of suffering, and connect all sentient beings with happiness and its causes.

As you gradually develop familiarity with these contemplations, you will feel their impact.

SEVENTH STEP: ASPIRING TO ENLIGHTENMENT

1. Analyze whether at present you have the capacity to help others become endowed with happiness and free from suffering.

2. Consider that in addition to providing temporary help it is necessary to educate beings so that they themselves can become enlightened.

3. Draw the conclusion that you must achieve enlightenment in order to remove the obstacles to knowing others' interests and dispositions, and to knowing which particular techniques are needed to help them.

4. Resolve to achieve enlightenment in order to help others to the fullest.

Switching Self and Other

1. Take this thought to heart:

> All sentient beings, through and through, are similar to me in wanting happiness and not wanting suffering. All of us want happiness and want to get rid of suffering. Therefore, how could it be right to have lust for some and hatred for others! I should help achieve happiness for all!

Then consider this:

> All sentient beings exclusively want true happiness but do not possess it. No matter whom I might consider in the realms of cyclic existence, they are undergoing the suffering of pervasive conditioning. Given this, whom could I single out to consider close! Whom could I single out to consider distant!

2. Imagine ten beggars, all of whom are equally destitute, and consider how groundless it is to have good feelings for some and not for others.

3. Imagine ten sick persons who are equally ill; how could you be close to some and distant from others?

HOW EVERYONE HAS HELPED YOU

4. Consider how everyone has helped you. All sentient beings have directly or indirectly provided services that have benefited you; regardless of their motivation they have been kind to you.

5. All the comforts of this life are dependent upon other sentient beings. Reflect in detail on how your food, clothing, residence, friendship, reputation, and possessions all come by way of other sentient beings.

6. Your present human life comes from moral actions in previous lives performed in relation to others.

7. Long life, freedom from illness, resources, creditable speech, and strength all come from moral actions in former lives.

8. Attainment of a good future life is based on moral actions performed in relation to sentient beings.

9. Morality is based on the principle that we must do no harm to others, thus other sentient beings are essential; without them you cannot perform virtuous deeds that keep them from harm. The virtue of refraining from killing requires other beings, as does refraining from stealing, sexual misconduct, and most other virtues. Without other sentient beings, these virtues could not be practiced.

10. Since morality is the very foundation of concentrated meditation and wisdom, even liberation from cyclic existence is due to sentient beings.

11. Attainment of Buddhahood relies on others, since the distinctive practices for achieving that state are love, compassion, and the altruistic intention to become enlightened, which come from taking notice of suffering beings and being moved from the depths of your heart to bring help and happiness to them. Hence we should respect them as much as we respect the Buddha.

12. Enemies are particularly valuable for cultivating love and compassion because anger destroys love and compassion, and the antidote to anger is patience, which can be practiced only toward someone harming you. Since enemies provide a valuable opportunity for practicing such forbearance and tolerance, they are very valuable, even kind.

13. Unlike a doctor who brings pain in order to help, an enemy harms you intentionally; this is how an enemy provides a chance to cultivate patience.

There Is No Good Reason for Being Egocentric

14. A suitable reason for considering only yourself worthwhile and neglecting everyone else simply does not exist. For both you and others are equally stuck in cyclic existence with the burden of a mind-body system driven by afflictive emotions and karma.

15. Both you and others are facing imminent impermanence and death.

16. Imagine ten prisoners who are about to be executed for the same crime; it does not make sense for one among them to be attached to certain prisoners and to be angry at others. The only sensible course is to be kind and patient with one another; it would be foolish to argue, making a distinction between "you" and "I."

17. Similarly, all of us have fallen under the influence of suffering, impermanence, and afflictive emotions. Given that this is our situation, what is the point of making a big deal about yourself and considering others to be beneath you!

The Disadvantages of Self-Cherishing and the Advantages of Other-Cherishing

18. Up till now, self-cherishing and its partner, ignorance, have taken up residence in the center of your heart. Despite drawing you into all sorts of actions to bring you happiness, these attitudes have only created a mess. You need to view self-centeredness as faulty from the depths of your being.

19. Now it is time to leave self-cherishing behind and take up cherishing others, to leave ignorance behind and take up the wisdom that realizes selflessness.

20. By looking after others, the Buddha perfected his own mind and body, providing for both his own welfare and that of oth-

ers, achieving perpetual bliss and the greatest possible ability to help others. We should do the same.

21. Though this might seem difficult to achieve, with time and effort it will happen.

That is the way to develop a sense of equality with others that motivates you to bring help and happiness to everyone everywhere.

Viewing Reality

1. All phenomena, whether external or internal, are empty of being truly established, empty of inherent existence.

2. No matter what you consider—visible forms, sounds, odors, tastes, and touches, or your own mind that is observing them—understand that these are empty of existing in and of themselves; they do not exist the way they appear.

3. To eradicate ignorance it is necessary to generate wisdom that contradicts it.

4. First the mind-body complex is misunderstood as existing inherently, and this leads to the misconception of "I" as being inherently existent. This, in turn, induces misguided actions that make for more rebirths, more suffering.

5. Based on the fact that we are mainly concerned with 1) the person, or "I," who acts, accumulates karma, and as a result experiences pleasure and pain and 2) the phenomena that are experienced, we can distinguish two types of ignorance: one that believes persons exist inherently and another that sees all other phenomena as existing inherently.

6. In truth, persons exist but without inherent existence, and this is called the selflessness of persons; when it comes to

other phenomena such as eyes, ears, body, mind, mountain, and the like, this is called the selflessness of phenomena. These two emptinesses are equally subtle.

7. It is necessary to differentiate between how phenomena appear to us and how they actually exist in fact.

8. Persons and other phenomena actually depend on thought, but when we interact with them we feel that there is something over there in and of itself, independent of being thought of, having all its capacities right in itself.

9. If it is actually there in its own right as it appears to be, then as you analyze it, it should become clearer and clearer, but it does not; you cannot find anything that exists in such a solid way. When you delve deep enough into its being, you are finally left with nothing to point at that is the object.

10. Even in sense perception, phenomena falsely appear concrete due to faults in our minds, and because of this false appearance, we are automatically drawn into conceiving that phenomena exist in their own right, much like assenting to false appearances in dreams. An unfounded appearance is taken to be true, and then we add many other attributes through improper, counterproductive thinking, creating a mess of afflictive emotions.

11. Due to this conflict between appearance and reality, the Middle Way School speaks of entities that create help, harm, and so forth, calling them "conventional truths"; then it speaks of the reality beyond these appearances, which is called "ultimate truth." In one object, such as your body, its appearance can be found by conventional valid cognition, and its mode of being can be found by final analysis.

12. Innate ignorance takes cognizance of any object, a person or any other phenomenon, and assents to its appearance as inherently existent, existing by way of its own character, existing as its own reality, existing as its own mode of being, truly existing, ultimately existing, existing without any conflict between how it appears and how it actually is.

13. When through meditative analysis you realize the emptiness of inherent existence, you understand that you and all other phenomena seem to exist one way but actually do not. You see phenomena as being like illusions, with a discrepancy between their appearance and the actual truth of their existence.

14. Viewing persons and things as having this conflict between appearance and fact, like a magician's illusions, will keep you from coming under the influence of destructive emotions.

15. To see phenomena as being like illusions, it is necessary first to analyze whether phenomena really do exist the way they seem to exist.

The Way to Analyze

Consider:

1. We are at the center of all our troubles.

2. It is therefore best to work at understanding our true nature first.

3. After that this realization can be applied to the mind, the body, the house, the car, money, and all other phenomena.

FIRST STEP: GETTING A HOLD OF THE SELF YOU STRONGLY BELIEVE IN

1. Imagine that someone else criticizes you for something you actually did not do, saying, "You ruined such-and-such," and points a finger at you.

2. Watch your reaction. How does the "I" appear to your mind?

3. In what way are you apprehending it?

4. Notice how that "I" seems to stand by itself, self-instituting, established by way of its own character.

SECOND STEP: DETERMINING THE CHOICES

1. Analyze whether the "I" that is inherently self-established in the context of the mind-body complex could have a way of existing other than being part of the mind and body or separate from them.

2. Decide that if the "I" inherently exists as it seems to, then it must be either one with or separate from mind and body.

THIRD STEP: ANALYZING ONENESS

Consider the consequences if the "I" is established in and of itself, as it appears to our minds. If it is the *same* as mind-body:

1. "I" and mind-body would have to be utterly and in all ways one.

2. In that case, asserting the separate existence of an "I" would be pointless.

3. It would be impossible to think of "my body," or "my head," or "my mind."

4. When mind and body no longer exist, the self also would not exist.

5. Since mind and body are plural, one person's selves also would be plural.

6. Since the "I" is just one, mind and body also would be one.

7. Since that mind and body are produced and disintegrate, it would have to be asserted that the "I" is inherently produced and inherently disintegrates, in which case either the pleasurable effects of virtuous actions and the painful effects of nonvirtuous actions would not bear fruit for us, or we would

be experiencing the effects of actions we ourselves did not commit.

FOURTH STEP: ANALYZING DIFFERENCE

Consider the consequences if the "I" is established in and of itself, as it appears to our minds, and if it is also inherently different from mind-body:

1. "I" and mind-body would have to be completely separate.
2. In that case, the "I" would have to be findable after clearing away the mind and body.
3. The "I" would not have the characteristics of being produced, abiding, and disintegrating, which is absurd.
4. Absurdly, the "I" would have to be either just a figment of the imagination or permanent.
5. Absurdly, the "I" would not have any physical or mental characteristics.

COMING TO A CONCLUSION

1. If in the first step you got a fairly strong sense of how the "I" appears to be self-instituting and how you usually accept that appearance and then act on the basis of it, analysis will in time reveal that this sense of "I" is unfounded.
2. When that happens, remain in vivid awareness of the absence, the emptiness of such an inherently existent "I," absorbing the meaning of emptiness, concentrating on the absence of inherent establishment.

VIEWING YOURSELF AS LIKE AN ILLUSION

1. Then, once again let your appearance and that of others dawn to your mind.
2. Remember a time when you mistook a reflection of a person in a mirror to be an actual person; it appeared to be a person but was not.

3. Similarly, all people and things seem to exist without depending on causes and conditions, on their parts, and on thought, but they do not. In this way, people and things are like illusions.

4. Reflect on the fact that within the context of dependent-arising you engage in actions and thus accumulate karma and experience the effects of those actions.

5. Consider the fact that the appearance of people is feasible within the absence of inherent existence.

6. When being viable and emptiness seem to be contradictory, use the example of a mirror image:

> The image of a face is undeniably produced in dependence on a face and a mirror, even though it is empty of the eyes, ears, and so forth it appears to possess, and the image of a face undeniably disappears when either face or mirror is absent. Similarly, even though a person does not have even a speck of inherent establishment, it is not contradictory for a person to perform actions, accumulate karma, experience effects, and to be born in dependence on karma and destructive emotions.

7. Try to see the lack of contradiction between being viable and emptiness with respect to all people and things.

Buddhahood

Consider:

1. It is impossible for the continuum of consciousness, which has a nature of luminosity and cognition, to ever be severed. When wisdom undermines ignorance, there is no condition that could oppose the continuation of basic mind.

2. Enlightenment is a state of freedom not only from the counterproductive emotions driving cyclic existence but also from the predispositions established in the mind by those afflictive emotions.

3. These subtle predispositions are latent forces within the mind that see to it that, prior to Buddhahood, whenever conventional phenomena come to mind, the ultimate truth is not manifest, and whenever the ultimate truth is manifest to your mind, conventional phenomena cannot appear.

4. This necessity of alternation is called the "defilement of apprehending the two truths as if they were different entities." Due to this limitation you are forced to switch between direct realization of the profound reality and paying attention to everyday phenomena, but when this defilement is extinguished, a single consciousness can take conventional phenomena to mind even while it is also directly realizing the ultimate truth.

5. It is then possible to simultaneously know everything, both the diversity of phenomena and their profound mode of being, emptiness. This is omniscience, a Buddha's "great enlightenment," which is purification from the sources of all problems and full comprehension of all that can be known.

6. This state fulfills your capacity to effect both your own development and that of others. You have overcome all problems and have achieved realization of all knowables, which means that you can bring about the well-being of others spontaneously.

7. At Buddhahood you attain the four Buddha bodies:
   - Your mind has from beginningless time been empty of inherent existence, and now that your mind is purified of all

defilements, the same emptiness is called a Buddha's *nature body*.

- Your mind, which formerly merely contained the *seeds* of the qualities of Buddhahood, is now a Buddha's *wisdom body*.

- Even in ordinary life, very subtle mind and the energy that drives very subtle mind are one entity, and now in the pure state of having completed the path this basic fact allows you to manifest in countless ways in forms appropriate to helping others. Among these forms is a *complete enjoyment body*, which, in accordance with earlier prayer-wishes, remains as long as space exists to relieve suffering through continuous altruistic activities for high-level practitioners.

- The complete enjoyment body, in turn, appears in myriad worlds in various *emanation bodies* in accordance with the dispositions and interests of sentient beings when the time is ripe; it also appears at appropriate moments throughout history as a "supreme emanation body," to teach the path to enlightenment (Shakyamuni Buddha was such a being).

Selected Readings

His Holiness the Dalai Lama, Tenzin Gyatso. *How to Expand Love: Widening the Circle of Loving Relationships*. Translated and edited by Jeffrey Hopkins. New York: Atria Books/Simon & Schuster, 2005.

——. *How to Practice: The Way to a Meaningful Life*. Translated and edited by Jeffrey Hopkins. New York: Atria Books/Simon & Shuster, 2002.

——. *How to See Yourself as You Really Are*. Translated and edited by Jeffrey Hopkins. New York: Atria Books/Simon & Shuster, 2006.

——. *Kindness, Clarity, and Insight*. Translated and edited by Jeffrey Hopkins; coedited by Elizabeth Napper. Ithaca, N.Y.: Snow Lion, 1984; revised edition, 2006.

——. *Mind of Clear Light: Advice on Living Well and Dying Consciously*. Translated and edited by Jeffrey Hopkins. New York: Atria Books/Simon & Shuster, 2002.

Hopkins, Jeffrey. *Nagarjuna's Precious Garland: Buddhist Advice for Living and Liberation*. Ithaca, N.Y.: Snow Lion, 1998.

——. *A Truthful Heart: Buddhist Practices for Connecting with Others.* Ithaca, N.Y.: Snow Lion, 2008.

——. *Tsongkhapa's Final Exposition of Wisdom.* Ithaca, N.Y.: Snow Lion, 2008.

Jordhen, Geshe Lobsang, and Lobsang Choephel Ganchenpa and Jeremy Russell. *Stages of Meditation.* Ithaca, N.Y.: Snow Lion, 2001.

Rinchen, Geshe Sonam, and Ruth Sonam. *Yogic Deeds of Bodhisattvas: Gyel-tsap on Aryadeva's Four Hundred.* Ithaca, N.Y.: Snow Lion, 1994.

Sherbourne, Richard, S. J. *A Lamp for the Path and Commentary.* London: Allen & Unwin, 1983.

Sonam, Ruth. *Atisha's Lamp for the Path: An Oral Teaching by Geshe Sonam Rinchen.* Ithaca, N.Y.: Snow Lion, 1997.

Sopa, Geshe Lhundup, and Elvin W. Jones and John Newman. *The Stages of Meditation: Bhavanakrama II.* Madison, Wis.: Deer Park, 1998.

Tsongkhapa. *The Great Treatise on the Stages of the Path to Enlightenment.* 3 vols. Joshua W. C. Cutler, editor in chief, Guy Newland, editor. Ithaca, N.Y.: Snow Lion, 2000–2004.

Wallace, Vesna A., and B. Alan Wallace. *A Guide to the Bodhisattva Way of Life.* Ithaca, N.Y.: Snow Lion, 1997.